*The Second Book of the Lamb*

# The Second Book
# of the Lamb

Peter C. Stone

Gabriel Press
Ventura, California

Published by:   Gabriel Press
                Post Office Box 5100
                Ventura, California 93003

ISBN 0-934469-02-4

Manufactured in the United States of America.

10 9 8 7 6 5 4 3 2 1

*Then I looked, and lo, on Mount Zion stood the Lamb, and with him a hundred and forty-four thousand who had his name and his Father's name written on their foreheads. And I heard a voice from heaven like the sound of many waters and like the sound of loud thunder; the voice I heard was like the sound of harpers playing on their harps, and they sing a new song before the throne and before the four living creatures and before the elders. No one could learn that song except the hundred and forty-four thousand who had been redeemed from the earth.*

—Revelation 14:1-3

# CONTENTS

Preface                                                                15

1.  Introduction                                                       21
2.  Reality, Pageant, and the Grand Purpose
    of Life                                                            23
3.  Intermediate Truth: the Basis of Religious
    Belief                                                             26
4.  Reincarnation                                                      29
5.  Thought and Mental Communication                                   32
6.  The Source and Purpose of the Scriptures                           34
7.  The Realm of God                                                   37
8.  Our Cultural Awareness of God                                      39
9.  The Lessons of Conscience                                          40
10. Theology and the Development of
    Consciousness                                                      41
11. The Pageants of Scripture                                          44
12. Man, the Brain, and Perceptive
    Communication                                                      46
13. The Growth of the Conscious Mind                                   48
14. The Shepherds of Man                                               50
15. God's Purpose for Consciousness                                    52

16. The Teacher is Still Learning   54
17. The Simulation of Conscious Knowing   55
18. The Development of Mature Perspective   56
19. The Malcontent and the Limits of Mercy   57
20. The Weaving of Consciousness   59
21. The Purpose of Time   61
22. Time and the Programming of Perception   64
23. The Illusion of Natural Law   67
24. Light and the Stars   69
25. Space Travel   71
26. Going Back in Time   73
27. The Two Facets of Time   76
28. Relativity   79
29. The Illusion of Distance   81
30. Parallel Universes   82
31. The Natural Reality   83
32. Multidimensional Being   87
33. The Oneness of Space   88
34. Sacraments, Salvation, and the Cross   90
35. An Example of Multidimensional Being   92
36. Knowing is Our Way   94
37. The Structure of Biblical Prophecy   96
38. The Mature Consciousness   99
39. Programming and Mass Social Response   101
40. Music and Art   104
41. The Organization of Perception   107
42. Images, Matter, and Genetic Processes   109
43. Primal Life Forms and the Evolution of Man   111
44. The Flood: Transition to a New Reality   115
45. God's Truth   118
46. The New Reality   120
47. The Revision of Earth   123

| | | |
|---|---|---:|
| 48. | Apparent Time and the Ages of Earth | 125 |
| 49. | The Redistribution of Consciousness | 128 |
| 50. | The Introduction of Disease | 131 |
| 51. | The Implementation of Society | 134 |
| 52. | Stress and the Optimization of Growth | 136 |
| 53. | Male and Female | 139 |
| 54. | Time and Space: Constructs of a Higher Realm | 141 |
| 55. | The Continuing Creation of Reality | 143 |
| 56. | Graduation: the Metamorphosis of Man | 145 |
| 57. | The Transfiguration Process | 148 |
| 58. | The Clarion Call | 150 |
| 59. | The Final Knitting of Perception | 152 |
| 60. | A Love You Can Feel | 154 |
| 61. | The Apparent Universe | 156 |
| 62. | The New Graduate | 157 |
| 63. | The Militant Masses and the Restructuring of Society | 159 |
| 64. | Satan and Evil | 162 |
| 65. | The Stress Crucibles | 165 |
| 66. | The Infiltrations of Mankind | 168 |
| 67. | The Coming of Christ | 171 |
| 68. | The Covenant with Abraham | 174 |
| 69. | The Maturing of Earth | 177 |
| 70. | The Revelation to John | 179 |
| 71. | The Christ, the Father, and Jesus | 182 |
| 72. | Love and the Creative Energy of God | 185 |
| 73. | The Sons of God | 187 |
| 74. | Confrontation and Mental Stress | 189 |
| 75. | Consciousness is What We Are | 192 |
| 76. | The Mature Mind and Its Continued Growth | 193 |
| 77. | Love's Ultimate Value to Man | 195 |

78. The Clergy                                          197
79. Prayer                                              200
80. An Enlightened Age Begins                           202
81. The New Knowledge, and the Brotherhood
    of All Living Creatures                             204
82. Political Process and the Control of Society        206
83. Cause and Effect Within Political Process           208
84. War, Strife, and Mass Conflict                      210
85. Mortal Confrontation                                213
86. Abortion, the Media, and the Activation
    of Mankind                                          215
87. The Hidden Message of the Scriptures                217
88. Dawn is Breaking Upon Man                           220
89. Welcome to Heaven                                   221
    Afterword                                           223
    Index                                               227

## REFERENCES

Unless stated otherwise, all biblical quotations are from the Revised Standard Version (Second Edition) of the Holy Bible. Reference is also made to the New King James Version of the Holy Bible (Thomas Nelson, Inc., 1984) and *The First Book of the Lamb* (Gabriel Press, 1987).

*Behold, the days are coming, says the LORD, when I will make a new covenant with the house of Israel and with the house of Judah—not according to the covenant that I made with their fathers in the day that I took them by the hand to bring them out of the land of Egypt, my covenant which they broke, though I was a husband to them, says the LORD. But this is the covenant that I will make with the house of Israel after those days, says the LORD: I will put my law in their minds, and write it on their hearts; and I will be their God, and they shall be my people. No more shall every man teach his neighbor, and every man his brother, saying "Know the LORD," for they all shall know me, from the least of them to the greatest of them, says the LORD. For I will forgive their iniquity, and their sin I will remember no more.*

—Jeremiah 31:31-34 (New King James Version)

# PREFACE

This work follows *The First Book of the Lamb,* which describes the remarkable events that began on the evening of October 24, 1983, with the communications of a spirit, or conscious entity. Several days later, having enjoyed many astonishing, intellectual discourses by our unseen visitor, my wife and I were literally shocked speechless when he announced that he was the Holy Ghost; that I was someone known as the "Lamb"; and that it was my task to prepare mankind for the coming of Christ.

He explained that he was the expected Christ, and that the role represented, for him, the culmination of a two thousand year tour of duty during which he had been in charge of God's school of earth—a school whose sole purpose is the creation and development of mature conscious beings. A school that was now being readied for graduation day.

As the weeks progressed, he revealed much, much more—about himself, about God, about the cosmos, and about the events beginning to unfold. I found myself led

15

along a daily path of instruction and communicative training that continuously grew and developed in both informational content and perceptual content; I literally found myself able to *understand* more, and then I found out why . . .

Since the initial contact, I have communicated with him each and every day. The communications, now entirely mental, are conducted as a conversational dialogue that is as clear and distinct as though he were a person speaking in a normal tone of voice from only an arm's length away. In addition, the dialogues are brilliantly colored by a very strong, electric, yet extraordinarily pleasant sensation that he induces within my nervous system as a signal of affirmation. The combined communicative paths feel, quite simply, like talking to someone who lives within me—sharing my skin, as it were—but someone warm, loving, benevolent, and immeasurably intelligent.

On May 30, 1984, using a slow, meticulous delivery easily amenable to handwriting, he dictated his first message intended for the world at large; pursuant to his wishes, that message now appears as the final chapter of *The First Book of the Lamb.*

Several weeks after that work was complete, he commenced the dictation of text on a regular daily basis, beginning with a brief period during which my secretarial skills were honed to the degree required. Within a matter of days I found myself easily and comfortably recording a delivery rate of perhaps one-third that of ordinary speech. Then, on July 6, 1984, he began dictating *The Second Book of the Lamb;* roughly two months later, it was complete.

Structured as a series of essays, his dictated text is recorded herein exactly as received; although I have been required to add punctuation and an occasional footnote, there have been no textual modifications unless specifically directed by him. The words are his, the emphasis is his, and the message is his. You will find it somewhat difficult to read in places, but believe me, it is eminently worth your while.

It should be noted in this regard that he has subsequently dictated almost three thousand pages of additional material, spanning subjects of such diversity as to astound the most erudite mind. Some of it is poetry, some of it is lovely prose, but most of it is information on our reality, our past, and the glorious purpose of our very being. It is dictated in a variety of linguistic styles that vary from eloquently simple to incredibly complex, from logically straightforward to sheer intellectual and perceptual challenge. His intellect is quite obviously without earthly bounds; therefore, if you find the material before you somewhat difficult to read, you can be certain he intended it so.

The text of this book, together with the concluding chapter of *The First Book of the Lamb,* represents his first written input to the system of man since he similarly dictated the Book of Mormon, approximately 150 years ago. In this regard, he has also explained that virtually identical communicative principles were employed in the transmission of the Koran and the original scriptures of both the Old and New Testaments of the Bible.

As you read these essays, you will begin to realize that a new age is quite literally bursting forth upon man—not in the ephemeral, distant future, but *now.* A new age in

17

which knowledge and love will rapidly supplant and replace the myth, supposition, and scientific ignorance of the past. A new age promulgated and decreed by God on high. A glorious new age for the *next* graduating class.

Peter C. Stone
September 24, 1985

*From this time forth I make you hear new things, hidden things which you have not known. They are created now, not long ago; before today you have never heard of them, lest you should say, "Behold, I knew them." You have never heard, you have never known, from of old your ear has not been opened.*

—Isaiah 48:6-8

# ESSAY 1: INTRODUCTION

*Received August 21, 1984*

This book represents a literal and historical milestone like no other to befall mankind, for it contains the first descriptive essays concerning the true nature of God and the cosmos ever provided to the society of man. I am the Holy Ghost. I speak and write through my Lamb, who has prepared this book. All the material contained within its pages is exclusively of my authorship, with his efforts strictly restricted to transcribing, editing, and preparing the material for public view. The pages of this book are holy, in the sense that they contain the written word of God in the same manner as have previous words of God been provided to mankind.

A new age is dawning upon man; an age of knowledge in which the natural laws of your apparent reality will soon give way to understanding of the true multidimensional cosmos and the wonders it contains. Mankind's society will alter as knowledge of the reality of God, the Sons of God, and the entire natural realm becomes commonplace within your cultures.

Mankind is entering an entirely new phase of being and

awareness wherein knowledge will truly overcome sin, evil, and the temptations of mortality—knowledge of the natural realm (Heaven); knowledge of God's loving, caring, but firm ways; knowledge of the very promise of godhood for those who learn their lessons well.

God has purposed earth, mankind, and the entire physical universe for the development of mature conscious intelligences who are self-sustaining, independent, immortal conscious beings. To them is extended the very promise of godhood itself as they develop hand in hand with their Creator and His heavenly staff.

God's hand is upon you and always has been, since the dawn of time. His nurturing ways provide the path for us to follow, and His love provides the wherewithal to follow it. He loves you all, as do I and the other inhabitants of the natural realm.

You are God's children, and we are your teachers.

# ESSAY 2

*Received July 6, 1984*

Western and Eastern religions share an overwhelming degree of compulsive, artificial causes at the roots of their structures. Both are structures intentionally created by the North Country[1] for the intentional purpose of creating an illusion of mortality while offering hope, somewhat vaguely, of immortality.

At the base of these structures is, of course, the reality of *pageant,* by which we are able to construct seeming realities for the benefit of our earthly pupils. Whereas these realities appear to be defined by impenetrable physical and mental boundaries, they are nevertheless carefully manufactured to correspond to and create the desired perceptions of their recipients.

Once a "reality" has been implemented, it is then only necessary to monitor and adjust its function as it progresses and develops with the flow of time. Furthermore, such monitoring and adjusting is greatly enhanced by the ease with which corrections may be implemented from within

---

[1]*North Country:* Biblical allegory term for the natural realm, or Heaven.

23

the North Country. Since all reality is in fact an illusion of reality constructed by a higher intellect using the stuff of actual reality, it is of no particular effort to cause maximal alterations in your apparent reality using only minimal effort within ours—the natural reality. How do we do it? With *pageant,* a subtle process involving modification of your reality through alteration and adjustment of your perceptions of reality—through changing your actual seeming knowledge of what you see, hear, and understand.

The process is, of course, intentional. With it we implement God's will by following a course of action which provides Him with what He wants: mature conscious intellects with which to create and inhabit a living, sentient cosmos. Consciousness has unlimited horizons within the framework He has provided; godliness itself is within the reach of all.

Consciousness implies more than mere existence; it is richer and more diverse in its attributes than ever conceived by mortal man. Consciousness is *knowing,* consciousness is *being,* consciousness is *perceiving.* It is intellect unbounded; it is service to the Creator; it is joyful existence; it is the pure pleasure of *being,* in the knowledge of pure and true harmony with His will. Consciousness is indeed all for a living being, with bodies and other physically living vessels providing only a road—a path—a direction—to the final state of conscious maturity: a self-sustaining, immortal, conscious intellect—a consciousness. An inheritor of God's infinite blessing upon His cosmos. A mote of self-sustaining wisdom, identity, and knowing that will almost surely become a god himself, some day. A being whose very essence is the delight and love of his Creator.

Love is the force by which your very reality is constructed, for it is a word merely representative of a pervasive, immensely fundamental force or energy provided and produced by God for the use of all. It is the very stuff of creation, with matter, energy, and other perceptions of your reality representing only interactive organizations of His creative force. Love is much more fundamental than mortal man has ever considered, and the learning of love much more important and significant to his development processes than ever imagined on earth.

The earthly perceptions concerning love, you see, are pageant; they are the elements of a carefully constructed program of education and development that provides in each newly mature consciousness a set of characteristics and perceptions that enable his very existence as a self-sustaining conscious intellect, free of the restrictions of physical reality. The earthly perceptions of love are therefore misleading, in that they do not accurately reflect the ultimate purpose or value of love. But since you are not intellectually capable of grasping the true goal of this course of instruction until you have reached conscious maturity (i.e., ready to graduate), it is therefore necessary to construct, within a framework of reality understandable by all humans, a set of love-related goals, attributes, and responses to which you *can* relate.

Physical life is a *simulator* in which the essential characteristics of a mature self-sustaining consciousness are synthesized through a program of manufactured realities. It is a training program specifically designed to teach and develop—to condition—to allow one to breathe in the natural environment of a loving God.

25

# ESSAY 3

*Received July 7, 1984*

It is therefore consistent with your reality that we introduce sufficient structure into your overall program of education that it embraces those elements you will require upon reaching conscious maturity.

Religion provides a combination of structures upon which interactive processes are constructed that serve to actualize or solidify the required program of learning. It is therefore a framework upon which structured programs of education are dependent for their form and function.

Western religion is, by definition, an interconnective framework or structure linking a variety of religious denominations or disciplines into a composite whole. In much the same manner is the Eastern religious framework constructed, whereby various religious belief entities combine to create an amorphous body of belief characteristics possessing a series of unifying themes or structures. "Gestalts" are thereby created of each, consisting of a body or mass of disciplined belief that contains elements which clarify and color the character and value system of the whole.

Cult religions participate in a unique manner to restrain, offend, redirect, and redeploy the directions and energies contained within the large organizations, or gestalts, of world religious belief.

It is undeniably characteristic of these gestalts that they contain, within structures unique to their function, not only meaningful truths but great quantities of meaningless literalisms (allegorical truths expressed by literal half-truths or nontruths) as major components of their structures. Further complications and unknowns are introduced through deception, distortion, and doctrine, all of which provide paths to the intentional insertion of nonmeaningful noise into the religious belief system.

Truth, per se, has little to do with the purpose and intent of earth's developmental structure for consciousness. Although it is implicit within the framework of a loving educational and developmental system to employ truth as frequently as possible, it is unfortunately not practical, nor in most cases even possible, to employ truth within the educational mechanisms of earth. The truth is so far removed from the understanding of consciousness when still operating at the earthly level that it is virtually incomprehensible. Wonderful—but worthless, if you are not sufficiently evolved intellectually to comprehend it. The system, therefore, must *simulate* the truth with a carefully structured educational process. The graduate of this process is the lowest level of consciousness that is intellectually capable of accepting, or even understanding, the truth of His system.

Truth, of course, is a misleading term in that it implies final truth, which is the manner in which the term is employed above. Given the reality of conscious intellects which are as yet incapable of accepting or understanding their final truth, "intermediate truths" may be constructed that *are* comprehensible to the developing consciousness. While not "final truth" in the fullest sense, these intermediate truths are the best that can be provided, commensurate with the understanding of the pupil.

Earth's religions are constructed upon intermediate truths—colorful simulations geared to draw one in the direction required that he may ultimately understand, comprehend, and actually participate in the marvelous final truth of God's creation.

And thus, upon these principles, was the basis of religious belief founded on earth.

# ESSAY 4

*Received July 8, 1984*

Eastern philosophy is based upon a deep-rooted knowing, within appropriate cultures, of reincarnation of the soul. Although modified and distorted to cause the individual to struggle to perceive the truth, reincarnation as a tenet has been successfully integrated into the eastern religious belief system.

It matters not whether the individual considers reincarnation literally, semi-literally, or in some personally defined way; it is the *perception* of reincarnation that counts. For as the tree grows, so grows its shadow.

Reincarnation, of course, is the primary principle upon which evolution, or maturing, of the individual consciousness depends. Although not structured according to principles inherent in any present eastern religious philosophy, its existence is nevertheless fundamentally true.

Providing not only measured experiences but also consequences to those experiences over a wide range of growth parameters, reincarnation offers the ultimate growth process: growth devoid of "baggage" associated with failure at lesser levels.

29

By the simple expedient of a sequential supply of appropriate new physical bodies, the individual consciousness can be provided with growth challenges (intellectually as well as perceptually) that are compatible with its unique personality, character, and rate of progress. And since the physical memory is intentionally configured to comprehend and contain only experiences and lessons of the individual physical life, the process is wonderfully dynamic and forward-going. Whatever an individual consciousness has learned and attained in a specific physical existence therefore becomes its new plateau for the subsequent existence. No memories of the past life, of course, but also no memories of the lessons of the past life which the growing consciousness might incorrectly perceive as pain and personal failure. Reincarnation preserves all that a consciousness has attained in a particular life and ignores all that has been endured to attain it. Attained plateau follows attained plateau, in a continuously growing chain of life experiences that ultimately produce a fully formed, mature consciousness—a graduate.

But the system also has its negative aspects for those consciousnesses who do not follow their prescribed course of instruction, for only by doing what the teacher requires does the student progress. Negative progress is therefore also possible; although not encountered often, it is a severe problem for those who prefer to act in a contrary manner to the dictates of their conscience and other internal perceptions, for it is through those very channels that one's guidance occurs. Positive growth of consciousness is almost assured, for reincarnational life experiences are carefully supervised from within the North Country, and guidance provided through conscience and internal perceptions of right and wrong. "Follow your heart, regardless" is therefore a dictum of success. Ignore it and your final life-plateau may actually decrease, although the incidence of such occurrence is very low. An unfortunate end awaits those who repeatedly, life after life, ignore their internal guidance; but for most the prescribed end is the beginning—of life immortal with God.

Physical life is therefore a series of existences in which one's consciousness—one's *self*—is grown, developed, honed, and in general made ready for mature adulthood as a self-sustaining conscious intellect in the natural realm provided by God. It is a preparatory sequence, a developmental process, a nursery-to-graduate school educational process that renders one complete and functional in the natural environment known as Heaven.

Physical life is also a long, hard struggle by which one's consciousness earns each and every achievement plateau it attains. Beginning at the level of micro-organic life and extending through multiple intermediate species to mankind, the physical reality sequence is both long and arduous. It is also *necessary,* for it represents the very heart and soul of a creative process developed by God to effectively mass produce others like Himself. And we are the beneficiaries of His effort; we need only participate in accordance with His wishes to attain godhood ourselves. But He had to invent the process, and now He benefits from His achievement by the very fact of our maturing selves. His delight is our delight in pleasing Him—by growing to be like Him.

# ESSAY 5

*Received July 8, 1984*

Western religious thought provides, as a basis of its character, knowledge or supposed knowledge of the existence of a prime Creator. While specifically organized around similar tenets, several aspects or segments of western theology also proclaim varying degrees of *communication* with this prime Creator. Known to the Christian as a loving God that projects emissaries of flesh and bone, and to the Hebrew as a formidable God of vengeance and fury, the fundamental allying factor in Western theological thought is *God,* pure and simple.

Although it would be obviously impractical to connect divinity to thought in the mind of the average person, it is nevertheless an important aspect of the natural reality that, indeed, thought does connect one to God. And the mechanism invoked is so pervasive, powerful, and fundamentally important that it is, for all practical purposes, the very heart and soul—the *essence*—of knowing, respecting, and actually experiencing the Creator.

It is, you see, an aspect of human awareness that represents a concurrent or equivalent characteristic of the pure

conscious intellect, for it is through the mechanism perceived by humans as thought that communication actually
occurs at the level of a mature consciousness acting in his
natural environment. Forming an important element of
the educational experience program on earth, the simple
sequential thought process normally considered by humans
as thought, i.e., "talking to oneself," is not thought but
communication—talking to *others*. And it is through the
simple expedient of not disclosing the source of discrete
sequential thought patterns that the North Country intentionally conceals and utilizes natural communicative
processes. And since the recipient intelligences are by
definition not fully developed, it is a simple matter to
configure responsive communications so that they appear
to originate within—as some unknown, reflective thought
process from the hidden and uncharted recesses of the
mind.

# ESSAY 6

*Received July 9, 1984*

The structure of Western religious belief rests upon an informed flow of data from the North Country that has continued over the centuries. Some of this data has been injected into the belief system by novel means, such as example, stress-injection, correlation, and several other interactive and dynamic means. Primary, however, is the means of written input by virtue of North Country infiltration of the physical system by advanced incarnate consciousnesses.

These consciousnesses are, as described in *The First Book of the Lamb,* Sons of God who have specially qualified for their missions on earth by virtue of express abilities developed over the ages. Such a consciousness is writing the very words I speak, for instance, as this present work is dictated by me directly from the North Country. Each and every word is mine, exclusively. He writes as I speak into his conscious mind, a process for which he has uniquely qualified through unimaginable training and preparation.

The body of thought and written information constituting the basic structure of western religious belief has been intentionally produced by us to create a confusing array of theological non sequiturs that serve to confuse and obfuscate the very issues they purport to explain.

Commonly perceived as inviolate truth, scripture is actually and predominantly concerned with the lessons that humanity must learn. It describes and explains the illusion of mortality in a way most advantageous to the growth of consciousness. It contains and provides comprehension of all that is to befall the maturing consciousness in a way that is consistent with both its present, current, physical reality and the perceptions it is beginning to develop. It assists the manipulation of perceptions as one is directed by internal guidance first to one perspective then the next. It intentionally contains opposing perspectives on many issues, such that internal guidance may correlate to the written scripture regardless of the nature and orientation of the guidance.

Above all, the scriptures are a tool to learning; a complex association of words and ideas that clearly explain basic principles and lessons, while not explaining—but only referring to, in an unclear and obfuscatory way—the more complex values and lessons of a more advanced pupil. The Bible, you see, and all other scriptures provided by us, is a means to an end. It is intermediate truth, as described earlier. It is information consistent with both the state of advancement of the pupil and his current need for correlation of internal guidance with the written word. And since such guidance varies remarkably as the target intellect develops, the Bible must also provide *confusion* to the advanced pupil. Regardless of the desire for perfection and truth which is obviously inherent in a seeker of wisdom, it

35

is nevertheless impossible, within the limits and boundaries of physical reality, to actually describe the Truth. So there are no literal answers within scripture—only *suggestions* to the perceptive, inquisitive, advanced pupils of earth.

The scriptures therefore provide yet another essential function, for as the advanced pupil finds fewer and fewer answers within God's word, he must rely more and more upon his guidance from within.

So as his progress advances him to the awareness of internal guidance and the wisdom of reliance thereon, so do his external sources of wisdom and guidance—i.e., the scriptures—fade away in value and content. He is forced to rely upon his internal guidance at that point, for it has literally taken over the function of teacher for the remainder of his educational experience. The Bible, or whatever scriptures he refers to, has become quite literally nonexistent, as though a cloud had developed about it through which one could see only darkly. For that person, the scriptures have lost their clear meaning. He is on *internal* control—and growing.

# ESSAY 7

*Received July 9, 1984*

Western religious beliefs are characterized by an understanding and acceptance of God as Creator, as omniscient and omnipotent, and as a God of truth. Unfortunately, these simplistic perceptions are not necessarily accurate, for they fail to consider that the realm of God is incredibly advanced in a complex and highly sophisticated manner that one must describe by using concepts of realities, time, and dimension.

Pure consciousness exists in a way that few humans perceive, for it is a sentient organization of a primary creative force maintained and channeled by God, our Creator. This force has been previously described as a love force, for in it we find an interactive process of existence wherein we not only prosper by and create with this force, but we are also nurtured by it in a way controlled by God. Loving, caring, and nurturing are the bread and butter of heavenly existence, and are also the elements of creation.

Only by accepting the environment He provides may a consciousness advance and mature, and someday be godlike himself. Earth's primary purpose is therefore the production of purposed conscious intelligences who are determined, heart and soul, to delight their Creator with their individual attainment of love, intellect, and caring.

# ESSAY 8

*Received July 10, 1984*

Western civilization is culturally attuned to God as a symbol of creative power through the use of processes that continually and constantly incorporate the necessary attitudes into society.

A means to an end, these subtle presences in Western civilization provide a direct means of incorporating into life's mainstream a positive "knowing" of the existence of a Creator. Whether conscious or not, this knowing is built upon a constantly flowing basis of input from the North Country. This input takes many forms, for it is not necessarily physical in most implementations. Again, as described earlier, most input to the system is through a flow of perceptions and ideas directly into the minds of the target recipients.

In such a manner is the desired notion of a prime Creator instilled into Western civilization, through the *minds* of its thinkers, writers, authors, motion picture producers, laity, students, restaurateurs, wrestlers, and agitators. The process, you see, is nonexclusive, for the goal is total—as contrasted with selective—infusion of the knowledge of God.

# ESSAY 9

*Received July 10, 1984*

The perpetual love of God represents an asset of mature consciousness that efficiently provides numerous beneficial side effects within the educative process. For example, our knowing of this final great truth enables the construction of safe programs of learning about areas of intentional distortion of character. If, for example, a perception is intentionally distorted so as to cause an entirely erroneous set of perceptions in the pupil, then it is possible to further construct a circumstance wherein the faulty perception will win, for the unfortunate pupil, consequences that reinforce the folly of the intentionally created false perception. At that point the faulty perception is allowed to fade in favor of a correctly oriented one, and the pupil is left with both a correct perception and also a full knowledge of the consequences of not perceiving his correct perception accurately. In this manner is his reliance upon "inner voices" developed and his attention to conscience as a source of guidance enhanced.

# ESSAY 10

*Received July 11, 1984*

Now we will address the question of the semantics involved in our preparation for the present structure of civilization.

Although both eastern and western cultures display a marked tendency toward sharing of resources among one another, this tendency does not extend to theological ideas and the structures they represent. For it is in marked contrast to commercial evolution that theological practice has grown in an uncharacteristically restrained way; i.e., there has been little formal cross-fertilization of notions, concepts, and ideas.

In other words, *knowledge* of the idea-universe characterized by things theological has been so pervasively absent in eastern and western cultures that the ideas they represent have been only barely polarized into a framework acceptable to the very limited target consciousnesses to which they have been aimed.

Although structured by disbelief, the basic notion of religious doctrine has always rested upon a foundation of revelation, enlightenment, and other similar sources of knowledge commonly perceived as mystical or otherwise alien in some way almost impossible to comprehend. Also, such sources often lack the unifying theme of similarity of content, therefore allowing the reader, student, or preacher using such source material an overwhelming sense of disproportion when considering the causes and effects reported as contrasted to the veracity of the source of the material itself.

Confusion and lack of substance were primary goals of the logical process involved with the origin of the theological belief system of man. For it is through the unique use of "non-information" that the targeted consciousnesses strive to seek knowledge, and failing that, suffer in an environment perceived by them as something less than knowing but ephemerally greater than not- or nonknowing. Such is the process by which perception is developed, through a carefully applied program of non-information coupled with a North Country-induced knowing of the existence of *something more*. In this way the consciousness struggles to understand, and failing that, struggles just to hopefully perceive. And eventually it does perceive, although not the thing it was trying to understand but a more substantive, significant *something* that was the original goal of the non-information process.

Further application and extension of this basic idea provides the logical framework and structure of the theological system devised over countless centuries at the expense of several ancient false starts in the system, for it was through the careful and selective application of structured non-information and almost-information that the primary growth pattern of perspective was originated and established.

Non-information is therefore a tool of great significance in the training and expanding of consciousness. With non-information the consciousness senses a lack that may be compensated for, it perceives, in some unknown way. It feels that if it tried harder to understand the non-information, that it would actually succeed to some limited degree. It does not understand more upon such "trying harder," however, but it definitely does *perceive* more. And perception is the stuff and essence of consciousness, for it is the warp and the weave of the final conscious fabric that does not strive to understand things—it *knows.*

# ESSAY 11

*Received July 11, 1984*

Notable exceptions to the practice of non-information abound; however, these exceptions exist in very calculated and specific ways. The major exception is in the area of educational allegory within scripture, wherein intentional pageants *literally* describe the desired information. Omitted, of course, is the notion of pageant, leaving the gullible consciousness free to accept, at face value, the literal rendition of the allegory. In this event, non-information has been replaced by a similar tool: nontrue or nonfactual information. This type of non-information is then a highly structured form of story which is specifically geared to advance some specific component of the growing perceptive framework of a young or developing consciousness. It is meant therefore as guidance—as an intentional, loving, but nevertheless literally untrue building block of perception. For it is perception, not physical fact or the accurate recording of it, that forms the basis of consciousness. Fact, reality, physical things may be created, but consciousness must be lovingly *grown*.

Yet another form of non-information utilized by the

44

North Country is "free information"—the sights, sounds, feel, and smell of one's environment. These elements gradually produce colorations of perception as they interactively combine and recombine with the world around one, and with the non-information skillfully applied, to produce and refine *fundamental* perception: perception that senses a knowing, as opposed to sensing an ability to "figure out."

Gradual, therefore, is the process of shifting a developing consciousness from the level of figuring out knowledge and relationships to knowing them. But it is this final stage of knowing—perceiving—that represents an almost complete conscious intelligence; one who is almost ready to exist substantially and self-reliantly in the natural realm of Heaven.

Knowing is therefore the final plateau of a physically incarnate conscious intelligence. It is the final step before eternal consciousness, eternal memory, eternal knowing— and eternity with God.

# ESSAY 12

*Received July 11, 1984*

Perhaps the most sought-after shred of knowledge in mankind is knowledge of the Creator, for in this knowledge inherently lies the Truth of the Beginning. Man, you see, is a comparatively recent addition to the grand production referred to as Creation—not only recent, but only a little different in many important ways from those who preceded him.

Man, you see, is an adaptive form of life specifically configured to house, contain, and implement the highest form of consciousness involved in the earth growth system. Functionally designed to permit large variations in programmable performance levels, and furthermore designed to alleviate potential management functions in the North Country, present-day man represents only the final form of a design in progress for ages.

Critical in the design of man is the brain—a larger-than-usual mass specifically configured to connect the individual consciousness to the physical body and, furthermore, to allow the implementation of both specific and general purpose control programs that essentially permit automatic or non-tended functioning of the educative process for large segments of the population and for long periods of time.

Also provided within the brain are communicative functions, which may additionally be programmed to enable or require specific levels of intervention and communication from the North Country. In general, such programs are functional only in highly evolved consciousness incarnations in which special attention is prescribed. Such special attention may range from a low-level insight provided to an individual to full-fledged communication, such as was invoked in the physical brain of the prophet who now writes my words. It may provide only occasional communication, and it may provide constant communication; again, depending on the growth program or role or purpose of the incarnation.

Perceptive communication programming is implemented on most advanced consciousness incarnations, wherein actual dynamic and interactive guidance is frequently provided through alteration of the recipient's perception of his immediate environment. Tidy, noninvasive, and highly effective as an educative tool, perceptive-level communication is the interactive method most widely used by the North Country. With it one can make a black situation appear to be white, so that the recipient responds to a perceived white. Upon discovering it is actually black, the recipient's remorse preserves and strengthens the perception of white or black in the future, through the expedient of *causing him to err.*

# ESSAY 13

*Received July 12, 1984*

Perceptive growth is the supreme goal of the consciousness development process, for it embraces many attributes, characteristics, and knowings that provide the operating framework of the adult, mature, conscious intellect.

For it is through perception that growth is actually achieved. It is the operative element that dynamically forces the growth of the conscious mind or intellect. It actually stimulates, in a way, the apparent growth of the whole, and furthermore regulates and organizes its growth through careful application of growth-regulating perceptions from the North Country.

Perception, you see, is all; within it lies most of the meaningful attributes of the self-sustaining conscious intellect. Sensing of the environment, knowing, knowledge, skill, caring—all are aspects of the primary perceptive conscious intellect. For when a mature consciousness knows information, knows sights or sounds, knows memories, or knows intellectual material, it is operative perception that provides and actually produces the knowing. Perception therefore is the crux of conscious intellect growth processes; it is used to stimulate, enhance, and guide growth, and is also the desired final product. At first it is externally applied or induced at the will of a superior intellect, or teacher, and finally it becomes an attribute of the target consciousness itself. Growth is thereby attained through this continual process of inducement of perceptions to actually *create* natural perceptions within the pupil.

# ESSAY 14

*Received July 12, 1984*

Regulating perceptions is therefore an important task for the North Country, for only by controlling the rate of perceptive growth is full consciousness optimally achieved. Regulation of growth rate is therefore an important duty imposed upon us by the Creator, and is invoked by Him within the natural responses of His system.

Regulation of perceptive growth is fundamentally an automatic process at the lower levels of mankind and in all lesser kingdoms. Only in median-and-above mankind does it impose a burden of manual (as it were) intervention upon those of us in the natural realm. For it is here, in Heaven, that the life achievement processes of upper-level mankind must therefore be carefully monitored, such that appropriate perceptive responses may be both taught and formed at a sophisticated, interactive, and highly dynamic level.

This task of tending the upper-level interactive development process is maintained in the domain and under the personal care of myself and a select staff of highly evolved conscious intelligences whose immediate responsibilities are similar to those of a shepherd with his flock. Differing only in the methods invoked to corral and correct the sheep, the work actually imposes similar responsibilities to the shepherd's role.

Perception—not wool—growth is the goal, however, so all intermediate goals and corrections are with an eye to this desired end result. And since physical reality is an illusory phenomenon that effectively serves as corral, limiting the boundaries of self-willed perception, growth of the perspective may be efficiently controlled, induced, and aided by constant modification of the apparent reality. Sheep know the existence of a corral, not its detailed design and construction; alter either and the sheep will not know their reality has been altered. Neither will a human, whose corral is his perception of reality, which is altered at will by the loving caretakers of God's impending graduates.

# ESSAY 15

*Received July 12, 1984*

Fundamental to the development of consciousness, therefore, is *purpose,* for it is through careful enunciation and clear statement of the goal that the educative program is developed and optimized. Purpose therefore implies a desired final state of being for the students to achieve following completion of their educative process, for it is through foreknowledge of God's ultimate purpose that the intermediate growth-attainment goals of consciousness are set.

God, you see, is lonely. An incredibly perceptive and capable super-intelligence, He purposes the growth and development of companions. He purposes and commands the evolution of skilled conscious intelligences like Himself. He purposes and commands a cosmos filled with intelligences with whom He can share His loving achievements and His caring ways. He purposes our very existence, purposes our ability to achieve godhood ourselves, and purposes companions with which to exalt His presence and that which may be purposed for Him by an even higher authority, of which we know but little.

Life is everlasting for a mature consciousness. It is dynamic, ever changing, ever growing, ever loving, ever creating, and a source of continued and unbounded joy. Our segment of the state-of-being spectrum is only that, however—just a segment. What wonders lie beyond the abilities and perceptive powers of God, we have yet to comprehend.

# ESSAY 16

*Received July 12, 1984*

What is foremost in the mind of man? God, creation—where did it all come from, and how did it all happen? And of these, God is the largest mystery of all. But mystery is allegorical for unknown, for uncomprehended, for never known. But God, you see, is not unknown; neither is He uncomprehended. God is a conscious intelligence just like all will be some day. *Super-consciousness, super-intellect* describe Him accurately in the framework of understanding you will have developed by now, for He is on a different point in the developmental spectrum than we. But it is nevertheless a point we can expect to experience personally if we perform our duties—His will for creation—well. By then He'll have achieved a more advanced level for us to struggle to attain; but we will, eventually.

Dynamic, growing, becoming and knowing more—this defines not only His system and its precepts, but also those who follow them. The teacher always knows more than the student, and the Teacher is still learning, Himself, more to teach . . .

## ESSAY 17

*Received July 12, 1984*

Given both a mental process and a conscious awareness, one can simulate the method of knowing utilized by mature consciousness. Pretend for a moment that you are aware of some bit of knowledge. Play with it within your mind until you are familiar with its pretended facets. Consider the entire bit of knowledge as a function of its facets, one at a time (remember—*pretending* that the knowledge mote exists).

Then imagine filling in the pretended mote of knowledge, such that its contents become known; then, occupy a portion of that knowledge, perceiving it, as it were, from the inside out.

Now, look inward and outward simultaneously. Imagine peering into the knowledge while aware of its external facets. Simultaneously peer outward from within, being aware of the facets as they appear from within.

You are both within and without the mote of knowledge, and as your perspectives merge into a single advanced state of knowing, the mote of knowledge becomes part of your conscious awareness. You *know* it, as a part of you.

# ESSAY 18

*Received July 12, 1984*

Complicated awareness patterns control the development of mature perspective, causing unstable realizations to slowly merge and condense into a concrete, uniform nucleus of perceptive understanding. For as one develops as a conscious intellect, one constantly acquires and accretes a variety of perceptions, both valid and invalid. As the growth continues, the invalid perceptions are dynamically tested through North Country intervention, one by one; and as the invalid perceptions become diminished, so are the valid perceptions enhanced until, finally, after thousands of years, all perceptions are valid, none are invalid, and the task is complete. A conscious intelligence has been formed; self-sufficient, capable of survival in the natural realm, and capable of unbounded growth.

A kernel of God-stuff, ready to sprout.

# ESSAY 19

*Received July 12, 1984*

Growth is a function of both native (i.e., achieved) intellect and the developmental effort expended by the North Country. Growth is unachievable through the conscious effort of the immature consciousness, and can be attained only by obedience to the internal messages of conscience—mankind's perception of North Country input.

Growth is therefore dependent upon following one's internal guidance and upon the actual receipt of such guidance, and here we maintain a relatively simple system to determine who receives the guidance required to grow and advance: He who listens to guidance receives more; he who does not, tends to receive less.

Although a system of infinite mercy would ideally provide the malcontent with whatever guidance he required to succeed, that is not the way God's system works. In one sense, perhaps, it lacks infinite mercy. A better term for His system would be *reasonable and excessive* mercy. Malcontent consciousnesses are not permitted to drain the available resources of North Country guidance and growth control. We give all that we can possibly give without damaging

the growth potential of those who do try—who do listen—
and who do what they are guided to do, regardless. These
are the real deservers of maturity and immortality, and we
do not shirk our obligation to their growth. Impartially
given is the remainder of whatever time and energies we
have to the recalcitrant and malcontent. We try as hard as
possible, but not to the detriment of the educative program
of the deserving.

And if a malcontent consciousness becomes intolerable
in his unwillingness to heed guidance and grow, the day
must inevitably come when there simply is no more effort
available to give him without harming one more deserving.
And when such a day comes, his last incarnation has
arrived—barring, of course, a last-minute reversal of
attitude.

A consciousness that lacks maturity cannot exist without
the supporting framework of a physical body. The malcontent who refuses to grow is not incarnated again; he will
cease to exist. And tears will be shed for him.

# ESSAY 20

*Received July 13, 1984*

Commonplace among humanity is the perception of "knowing" within the self or psyche. Although the perception is common, however, understanding of the mechanism eludes both perceivers and thinkers.

For it is by perception itself that the knowing occurs, completely overshadowing any logical processes participating in the perceptive scenario. The perception of knowing is therefore a perception of a perception, an effect that illustrates and exemplifies the developmental goals of the entire educative process for consciousness. For as the conscious intelligence develops its own inherent perceptions, they are frequently blocked from the awareness of physical consciousness by virtue of individual brain programming; i.e., the student may have the perceptive ability as a part of his natural consciousness, but he may not be aware of it in physical reality.

Inherent in the educative process then is the notion of multiple or nested perceptions, wherein complete perceptive abilities are formed within the developing consciousness without accompanying perceptions of their existence.

59

Then, in an organized way, higher-level perceptions are formed which finally link, or include as elements of their structure, the previously formed and completed perceptions which have in effect been waiting for inclusion and incorporation into a larger, or "linking," perceptive mechanism or framework.

These nested levels of perception may be developed almost entirely free of conscious awareness on the part of the physical self, for it is not until the sequences are complete—the perceptions within perceptions within perceptions—that conscious awareness of their existence is allowed to link to the level of physical conscious awareness. And even then, the perceptions of the awareness of these faculties may be intentionally clouded or obscured, or perhaps even completely disallowed, until the remainder of the perceptive framework has been developed to a similar degree.

And so it continues, one layer of perspective and perception at a time. Nesting, linking, correlating, organizing—until the framework and the structure are complete, at which time full awareness is allowed to be realized by the consciousness, and maturity has been achieved. A new graduate is ready to meet his Creator.

# ESSAY 21

*Received July 13, 1984*

Definite boundaries exist in the design and implementation of a consciousness development program. One of the most stringent limitations one must observe has to do with the concept of interactive connecting of perceptive awareness cells, for it is at this primitive level of consciousness—the "building block" level—that the greatest number of constraints appear. It is at this cellular level of consciousness that the greatest care must be taken, for it later becomes the very fabric of the developed conscious intelligence.

Time then becomes an important interactive criteria, for the linking of perceptive cells must continue at a carefully controlled rate of progress, while simultaneously interconnecting or linking other portions of the conscious intellect and also creating some of the base (cellular) perceptions themselves. The entire education and development program for a specific consciousness must then be a carefully considered component of his growth implementation process at any one instant. Unfortunately, not all of the base perception cells can be developed at the beginning of the development process, for several are sufficiently advanced in nature as to require the prior existence of a reasonably well-advanced consciousness in order to have sufficient native perception to synthesize the desired advanced cellular perception. Once synthesized, this cell can be linked to other perceptive frameworks and can also be used to implement the creation of even more advanced perceptive cells.

The element of time is therefore key in the implementation of consciousness development, and for this very purpose does the current framework of time, as a restraining dimension, even exist. Time, you see, is a fabrication—a *pageant*—of the North Country. It is a way of synthesizing a consistent reality that enables the organization of succeeding or subsequent events into an automatic, nontended structure. In other words, it is the operative mechanism by which consciousness can develop and grow in such large numbers without the need for North Country intervention at an impossible-to-attain level. Time is the physical reality perception of a controlling mechanism to achieve the required organization of events. Its existence is therefore a pageant in which all other aspects of your experienced physical reality are caused to concur. It is a *fabricated, unnatural,* natural law. It does not exist beyond the framework of physical reality, for it serves one purpose and one purpose only—it organizes the consciousness development process. It need not be, and is not, invoked at any other level of existence. It is a pageant—a construct of your physical reality—and a nonexistent restraint in the natural reality.

Immortality follows naturally when the operative organization mechanism of physical reality is removed, for time is transparent—nonexistent—in the natural realm of consciousness.

Immortality, you see, is *natural.*

# ESSAY 22

*Received July 13, 1984*

The structure of time is therefore a function of the sequential growth processes involved in the consciousness development process. Viewed as a three-dimensional interaction restrained by the flow of time, the process lacks clarity to one currently within physical reality.

But imagine, for a moment, that time is a coordinate axis in a system of four concurrent physical dimensions. A being within the physical system could then view, comprehend, and furthermore manipulate a latticework of interactive physical phenomena all portrayed as physical elements within the physical dimensions. And it is by a simple stretch of imagination—of perception, actually—that the natural structure may be viewed from within three-dimensional physical reality. Reality, you see, has more than three dimensions. A fourth—time—has been included in your physical reality system to implement measured and complex organizations that lead to mature conscious intellects. Time is therefore a restrained dimension in your reality, whereby you are caused to perceive events in a measured way as

64

you artificially progress moment by moment, coordinate point by coordinate point, along a restraining fourth axis in your system of reality.

Time, as a natural dimension, is no different than length, breadth, and height; it is your *perception* that is restrained. And not only is your perception restrained, it is forced by programming to proceed along this restraining coordinate axis in a methodical, programmed way. And so is all of physical reality thus restrained, providing not only the desired organization of events concerning the development of consciousness, but furthermore creating illusions of motion and other seeming manifestations of a "natural" three-dimensional universe.

Electrons, for instance, seem to be in motion; they seem to have properties such as charge and mass; they seem to follow a natural order. But at the heart of these perceptions is the fact that they are perceived while progressing along yet another axis of perspective in a completely controlled manner of which you are unaware.

Your view of natural processes is then distorted by this restraining phenomenon upon your perspective, much like the distortion of a moving scene through the moving aperture of a focal plane camera. Natural processes are not the complicated, almost unknown phenomena you perceive. They are something inherently simple; your perspective quite simply lacks knowledge of the universe in which you exist. You are *programmed* to perceive the time dimension in an artificial, structured, and intentional way. Time really exists as a dimension; it is your perception that is an illusion. It is your perception of time that creates the illusions of natural law. It is your programming regarding time that effectively separates your reality; that renders the North Country physically indeterminate; that creates, within our natural reality, the physical, three-dimensional, restricted realm in which you exist.

ESSAY 23

*Received July 13, 1984*

The concept of sequential events is then the key to understanding the implementation of time as a restrictive, automatically regulating dimension. Imagine a three-dimensional system containing a sphere suspended in midair. Imagine perceiving only two dimensions, length and breadth, while progressing upward in a measured, automatic, sequential way. As you rise to the level of the underside of the sphere (remember—you are not aware of rising) you view a large dot. As you rise further, the dot grows to a disc. As you rise to the center of the sphere the disc grows larger, and then, as you rise above the center, it grows smaller again, until it disappears.

Your perspective during this journey has undergone continuous modification without your conscious knowledge as you have incrementally proceeded up the third dimension (height) in an unconscious, unaware manner. You have perceived what must be a natural law in your two-dimensional world: dots become discs and then dots again, only to disappear.

And that is exactly what happens in three-dimensional

reality as your perspective is automatically and unconsciously incremented along a fourth natural coordinate axis. Your natural laws are an illusion, a byproduct of this programming. Their existence is not real but only an illusion of perception. Complicated structures as perceived in physical reality are generally simple organizations when viewed with the programming deleted—when viewed without artificial modification of perspective. When viewed naturally.

The stars are an example of this phenomenon—this alteration of perspective—in action. Imagine a cosmic energy source. Imagine it varying in intensity along some imaginary fourth physical axis. Imagine your perspective being incremented along that axis, quite unconsciously. Imagine viewing the birth and death of a star, that never really happened.

# ESSAY 24

*Received July 13, 1984*

So-called "relativistic" phenomena are actually characteristics of the perspective modification program in action, for when one views, in physical reality, a heavenly object at great distance, one is not viewing an object at great distance. One is not even viewing an object at *any* distance, for distance itself is a characteristic byproduct of the time program wherein the physical reality perception of distance has to do with the amount of time something of known characteristics requires to traverse it.

But time, you see, is an intentional perspective obtained within three-dimensional physical reality through a program that increments along an additional physical axis in a preprogrammed way. Time as viewed or perceived in physical reality is therefore an illusion; it simply does not exist at any level of perspective wherein the program does not function.

Time therefore subjects distance to analytical processes within physical reality. And when it comes to interstellar phenomena, light becomes the yardstick to which time is compared.

And what is light? A massless object? A wave? No, light is neither. Light is the physical reality perception (perceived as one is unconsciously incremented along a fourth physical dimension) of natural energy within the cosmos. It does not travel across space at specific speeds, allowing measurements at great distance by mathematical analysis. It shows none of the properties upon which astronomical analysis depends, for it is not what it seems.

Light, you see, is the natural creative energy of the cosmos, viewed from the perspective of an unconsciously incremented physical axis. It exists. But it is observed by the individual in physical reality as something that travels and appears to have strange properties. It does not travel; your perspective travels along its length. Light *exists*.

The interstellar distances of the cosmos are illusion; they are not real. Light viewed from earth is the creative force of the cosmos flowing in and around the planet and its neighboring bodies. It is the very stuff of which the planet is composed, witnessed by its inhabitants in a sequential manner, as a result of their programming, as a stream that has traveled for eons.

It has not traveled for eons; it simply exists. It is the *stars* that do not exist, for they are simply representations—illusions—complex images resulting from the unconscious incremental control along a dimensional axis that precludes awareness of the natural environment.

The stars exist at no specific distance, for they are not really there; only their images exist as complex programmed representations—illusions—of the elements required to contain, or *apparently* contain, your reality. The stars do not exist; only the energy is really there.

It is God that you see at night.

# ESSAY 25

*Received July 14, 1984*

Now is the time to address one of the most outstanding aspects of the universe we live in, but rather than extend our perceptions to yours via allegory, a straightforward description based in your reality is a more appropriate approach.

Time, you see, is a complex effect created by our intentionally incrementing one axis of your four-dimensional reality in a programmed, step by step way. It therefore produces the effect of divorcing normal distance perceptions from the perspective of natural dimensional processes. In other words, time inclusion creates a false (or restrictive) perception in three-dimensional reality that distance is absolute.

Distance is not absolute; it is dependent upon the relative orientation of fourth-axis properties or characteristics. Much as the relative distance of two points in a three-dimensional world is dependent upon the third dimensional axis, so does the inclusion of a fourth dimensional axis similarly affect the real separation of the points.

Time flow is an alterable, non-natural perception of

reality. Recognizing its nature and basis in the modification of perspective, it can be *un*modulated to gain surprising effects within three dimensional reality. These effects would imitate normal or natural spatial behavior in the natural reality for the apparent interval during which they would be allowed to predominate.

The time modulation function, you see, is not necessarily sacrosanct under all conditions. Given correct guidance, perceptions, and training, also North Country cooperation, it is possible to realize, in the domain of three-dimensional physical reality, some of the freedom associated with the natural, multidimensional reality.

Given this option, distance may become nonlimiting upon humanity. Given this option, brief experiential samples of the natural laws which pervade our multidimensional reality could yield enormous benefits of learning. Space travel, you see, is not a matter of time and distance.

It is only a matter of cooperation.

# ESSAY 26

*Received July 15, 1984*

Placing one's thoughts within the perspective or orientation of time can yield informative perspectives regarding the true or natural reality. For example, one can imagine a world in which time travel exists as a commonplace leisure activity. If one existed in such a world, one would expect, on the surface, to be able to move freely—at will—within time, while remaining at the same physical location.

But what of the Paradox? What happens to the present if you alter a past event while it is your temporary present? This simple thought-game has tantalized mankind for centuries, kept alive philosophically by the perception (induced by us) that something is there—*something*—if only it could be discerned!

Time, you see, is not a natural law; it is an intentional modification of perspective regarding a dimension (or coordinate axis) of natural space. It is not a matter of events occurring, then almost magically ceasing to exist, only to be followed by succeeding events. Time does not actually work that way.

The experience and perception of time is an intentional

illusion, developed intentionally and specifically as a way of organizing the myriad interactive requirements and complexities of the consciousness development process. Time therefore—or rather the manner in which it is perceived by living beings in physical reality—does not exist in the manner assumed. Once again, it is not a natural process or law. It is, however, an intentional modification of your perspective of a natural physical axis. What you, as a living earth being, perceive as time is a three-dimensional physical reality in which your perspective is sequenced, in an automatic and non-tended way, along the fourth physical axis of your reality.

Certainly you are not capable, within your present operative framework, of going back in time. If you were, however, caused to be capable of perceiving the natural relationship of dimensions, you would be surprised, pleasantly, by what you would discern.

You would see a physical reality in which the time-modulated axis was simply a static, physical, nonmodulated law of nature, as it were. You would see objects as continuums of interactive energies, progressing and developing from one state of being to the next in an interactive, sentient, and very *alive* manner. You would perceive the reality of consciousness in matter, for it would look alive, growing, changing, to your uneducated eyes. And indeed it is sentient, low-level consciousness—alive, moving, changing—in the natural realm within which all physical reality exists.

Amorphous, interactive, alive, changing—all typify the nature of the natural physical reality. So if the imaginary time traveler were to actually go back in time, which is possible through modification of axis-modulation perceptions, he would not find the remembered past, for it would be only a memory, an illusion.

All is alive—a living, sentient, conscious organization of energy into physical reality manifestations of matter and energy. All is changing, maturing, developing. And your perspective of the present is a contrived view from a specific, constantly changing point on a fourth physical axis; a "slice" of reality, wherein the real, living conscious organizations which you view (seen through your intentionally limited perspective as quiescent matter) are constantly changing, altering, and composing to construct for you the reality you require.

The past does not exist; only a memory of a specific slice of reality at a specific point on the fourth axis. But even that has changed now, as you are incremented along, quite unconsciously, to incur the organization you require at your present point.

The past exists, of course, in the sense that it represents a physical coordinate within the natural system of reality. But it doesn't look like it did when you were there.

## ESSAY 27

*Received July 15, 1984*

Total and complete control over the time perspective experienced by those existing in physical reality is thereby achievable through simple modification of perspective in a manner consistent with the desired rate perception of succeeding events. Even as one supposes momentum to exist, so will one assume time to exist, especially when confronted with no evidence to the contrary.

Time, as perceived by man, consists of two separate and totally different perspectives of actual reality—not one. Separate the two and the conceptual process becomes more akin to the truth of the phenomenon. First, consider time as a sequence of subsequent events, intentionally caused (and caused to be experienced) by the North Country incrementally moving your perception along an axis of reality. These events actually happen in the sequence experienced, and become part of your conscious experience.

The passage of time, therefore, is considered commonly as a sequential series of realities occurring at some regular rate. This notion by itself is relatively accurate if restricted specifically to the notion of *subsequently experiencing successive realities.*

The second common interpretation of the time phenomenon is associated with the quantitative effects of time, as perceived on earth. Measurements of so-called "natural properties" of matter and energy are referenced to time, as are myriad other characteristics observed by seekers of knowledge. Unfortunately, these observations and measurements have only limited value, in that their accuracy—their very claim to existence—is based upon the dynamic processes observable *but not realized* on earth that are caused by the incremental successive manner in which your physical reality is constructed and continually modified.

Many observed physical processes involve the notion of time as a yardstick or point of reference. Time, when referred to in this way, involves the actual *process* of incrementing your perspective along a fourth coordinate axis in order to create the illusion of independent reality about you. Actually, however, the rate at which your reality is altered is a function of your current perceptive ability, and has no other absolute reference. Should time be considered as absolute in a quantitative sense, then one has based absolute measurements upon a reference that is not real.

The perception of time somehow being related to natural law has brought about the idea of relativity, wherein the apparent speed of radiant or electromagnetic energy is related in some intangible way to time, or more specifically, to the cessation of time (Einstein).

A more accurate representation is obtained, however, when one recognizes that the apparent speed of light is really a function of the rate of successive coordinate points—or rate of subsequent realities—that we impose upon you. Relativity will always hold for you, for no matter how "often" we increment your realities, your perception of time will be unchanged, and your perception of relativity will be constant. The speed of light actually has to do with your perception of your incremented-coordinate reality. The apparent rate of travel is caused by your motion in terms of subsequent realities, not the motion of light.

Relativity is not a mysterious relationship of a more mysterious natural universe. It is simply an observation of the invisible, imitation reality we have constructed for you. It is the dog viewed from the perspective of the tail.

# ESSAY 28

*Received July 15, 1984*

Cumbersome initially, the idea of relativity provides several interesting and highly evocative observations on the physical, or actual, implementation of your reality.

Time, as described earlier, exists as two separate meanings, the first being the qualitative sensation of succeeding events or experiences. The second is the quantitative sense, in which science attempts to measure and consider the observed universe in terms of a quantitative, ephemeral, but seemingly absolute thing called time. Time, in other words, is perceived to represent a natural law of some sort that must surely—someday—yield to analysis and experimentation.

Modulating the fourth physical axis perception in a totally artificial manner, we *create* your perception of reality totally within the natural reality in which we all exist. We *modulate* your perception of reality by allowing you to only perceive the fourth coordinate axis one coordinate point at a time, and in a rigidly sequential manner.

In this manner is your reality separated from ours, and in this manner is it contained within ours, such that your perceptions, deductions, and observations are easily comprehensible by us.

Your reality exists as a rapid series of three-dimensional slices of a natural four-dimensional physical system. Your perception of reality is incremented in an automatic way that causes successive realities to blend into a reality-stream of awareness.

And it is this mechanism of incrementing your reality perception along a fourth coordinate axis that creates the phenomenon you view as relativity. Time and mass are dependent, in your experience, on relative speed. Should the rate of reality increments come close to the rate of a physical three-dimensional object, distortion in the physical mass of the object would begin to occur as it approached the limiting ability of the three-dimensional incrementing system to resolve matter.

Relativity defines the *resolution* of your reality.

# ESSAY 29

*Received July 16, 1984*

The coordinate axis upon which such perception-incrementing modulation occurs provides the illusion of distance and speed, but in the natural realm this illusion is replaced by the natural *un*modulated perception of the fourth coordinate axis. Time, space, and distance are not functionally separated in the natural reality. Distance is an illusion of your fabricated, sequential slices of reality. Distance is itself ephemeral here, for it is a concept one must comprehend by reducing degrees of freedom of motion. Separation exists fundamentally among different points in three dimensional space which are actually connected by the fourth coordinate axis of natural space.

We do not travel or move from one point to the next. We *are* at one point, then we *are* at the next.

# ESSAY 30

*Received July 16, 1984*

Characteristically appearing as parallel universes to philosophers engrossed in time studies, it is widely anticipated that matter exists at more than one level and at more than one time.

Although inaccurate, the idea does possess plausible corollaries in that matter actually does exist outside your reality, and so does reality. But not just another reality—the *real* reality.

And since prosperity of thought develops from such notions, it is proper to reward these thinkers with kudos for insight, for although they are not correct, they nevertheless have perceived the tenuous *something* that actually exists: the natural, multidimensional reality. The *real* world.

# ESSAY 31

*Received July 17, 1984*

Now one could conclude from the preceding statements that the "real world" is one of properly arranged realities, each individually composed in a manner similar to the present *now* you are experiencing.

For many, the preceding statements would include the understanding or notion of a different reality—of a different, alien reality or world in which everything appears hopelessly alien and impossible to describe.

Since the truth lies between these extremes of interpretation, it is appropriate to consider the manner in which inhabitants of this real world actually view their surroundings in terms of their prior awareness of existence in your contained reality.

For to them, it is a matter of *more* reality, as opposed to different. Certainly it is different—much different, in fact, but the differences are not in conflict with the reality you now experience. The differences explain and augment your reality, producing or constructing (in a manner of speaking) an even more natural, more perfect, more explainable and understandable reality than that in which you presently exist.

Reality, you see, is only a matter of perspective. Having developed your conscious perceptions among others in a three-dimensional world, you will certainly find some surprises here. But they are happy, delicious surprises in which you savor reason and knowing and understanding, at long last, of the reality you have left behind.

Common among such responses is the one associated with love, as it is somewhat loosely referred to here. Love enables the very stuff of our existence; it is awesome in its far-reaching implications, for it is found to be rooted in the very creative process of God. With it one comprehends the fundamental interrelating ways of God's universe and His plan. One also comprehends the use of love as an organizing, structuring energy guided by the will of conscious intellect. With it, you see, one creates matter, energy, life itself, where indicated by the Master Planner of the cosmos.

With love one structures and organizes perception to create sentient, responding masses with which to create, in turn, matter itself. With love one forms the image of matter, and then with love fills the image and makes it real, in three dimensions. With love one creates—loves—*is.*

God-force, love, or whatever you are pleased to call it, love truly conquers all; it *is* all.

When one is mature as a consciousness, one has then developed the capacity to incur control of the very God-force love implies. Not known or realized on earth, this control development is inherent in the consciousness growth process. With it one creates, communicates, loves, lives—*worships* his Creator, who reciprocates then with only more love than before.

A remarkable force, love provides infinite power, infinite ability, and infinite grace while employing them. It is the very essence and stuff of God.

Given a reality in which creation occurs rather commonly, one must anticipate more differences from the familiar physical reality than simply the addition of a single dimension to space. It is far, far more. It is *infinite* dimensions, the existence of which are not even philosophized on earth.

Dimension, you see, involves degrees of freedom. It is being aware of properties of natural space; it is being at various points—or other organizations of lesser dimensions—simultaneously. Growth of perception involves dimensions of being in which, as your perspective grows, so does your potential state of being. It means not only perceiving two places at once, but being at one, then being at another; or, as you advance, being at both.

Then, as perspective growth continues, your prior beings organize into an even larger perceptual structure, to where you not only simultaneously perceive more, you *are* more. You are also capable of being within more, whether points, solids, or more complex organizations of time and space.

God is everywhere in the natural realm. Not because He is physically big, but through an advanced state of being and perspective. He is everywhere at once similar to a human perceiving all portions of a structure, such as a small building, at once.

Dimensions are infinite, and therein lies the promise and the perception of godhood. Continued growth continues the perceptive framework through additional dimensions, or degrees of freedom of perception. And with advancing perception comes, for the mature conscious intellect, advanced states of being.

Earth is but a nursery; now the fun starts.

## ESSAY 32

*Received July 17, 1984*

Connected with the idea of dimension is the concept of "being," in which one is capable of actually experiencing, controlling, existing at and perceiving more than one thing (whether point, solid, or complex organization of advanced dimensions) at a time.

Learning to be at two locations within three-dimensional reality is mastered quickly by the average newly matured conscious intellect. Stretch the concept a bit and one has three locations, then an organization of locations, then locations in and outside of your reality. Then add more complex organizations of reality and dimensions, and someday you too may be capable of existing everywhere.

Just like God does now.

# ESSAY 33

*Received July 17, 1984*

Now we will return to the topic of relativity, or time and space. For now that we have described the infinite nature of dimensions, the actual nature of your reality construct becomes perhaps a little easier for you to comprehend.

Space, you see, is composed of dimensional plateaus surfacing appropriately to perform their part in your apparent reality, then giving way to others more suited to the reality segment. It is not time, per se, that composes the elusive fourth axis of natural reality which we incrementally modulate; it is a *composite* of advanced dimensions of being in which space, distance, and time merge at a single point of perspective or being-awareness. Modulating—or incrementing—your reality through discrete subsequent values of this composite dimension (therefore more than one contribute) creates the illusion of space-distance-time within a reality which actually experiences none of these as limiting characteristics.

Freedom of conscious motion in the dimension we modulate creates a oneness of space wherein one can be at various locations in space simultaneously. It "wraps" space and time into a single point of perspective and being, and then "unwraps" it as your selection of simultaneous space emerges in your conscious intellect.

And this is just a mere example of the ultimate capability of conscious intelligence. Remember—the current system was developed before the earth was created.

# ESSAY 34

*Received July 17, 1984*

Characteristically adamant concerning notions of time, space, and reality remain the theological practitioners of planet earth, for to them is entrusted—or so it appears to them—the keys to the salvation of the souls of man.

To them is entrusted a far more important role than that of mere salvation, which is almost guaranteed for all who follow their conscience. To them is given the task of confusion; hopefulness; non-information and almost-information; caring and nurturing of the inner self; succor from the ravages of Edom[1] and Moab.[2] To them are given the keys of the kingdom in a rather novel sense, for they are the implements of God's carefully constructed program of stress, confusion, non-information, and *something greater* that causes men to struggle and strive to perceive more.

And thereby does man grow; not by the cross, not by the sacraments, but by struggling to perceive God's will in

---

[1]*Edom:* Biblical allegory term for the stress crucible associated with medicine and medical technology (described further in Essay 50).

[2]*Moab:* Biblical allegory term for science and technology (defined in Essay 65).

the midst of chaos, confusion, and non sequiturs in abundance.

The theologian of earth is typically a strong follower of God's will, for no man is as keenly aware of the inequities, non sequiturs, and failings of the religious structure than the very one who preaches it.

Yet something drives him on: an inner knowing that there is something more, something big, something incredibly *wonderful,* and if he tried harder perhaps he could somehow glimpse just a portion of the wonder he knows is just beyond his ken.

Platitudes appall the caring shepherds of the faith, but there is little else to offer—nothing *solid.* And so they hope, eternally knowing there is something more, and eternally infecting their flocks with the same unknowing hunger of something more—something *big*—if they could only perceive it!

# ESSAY 35

*Received July 18, 1984*

Perhaps another view of the structure of reality would prove helpful to those lacking positive perception of the preceding descriptions, for it is an entirely enviable person who can grasp such concepts succinctly and easily. Requiring an inner knowledge or awareness in order to comprehend at all, these concepts do not lend themselves to one who is not extremely mature in the sense of his conscious intellect.

Imagine, if you will, a field covered in clover, with flowers growing here and there. Imagine being at one location in the field, perhaps enjoying a flower's fragrance. Look up from your imagined location at a cloud overhead, and imagine yourself as *being* the cloud. Now imagine yourself as both cloud and yourself at once, connected perhaps by an invisible network of something that enables you to stretch between the two while preserving the sensations and awarenesses of each.

Now imagine the cloud lowering itself to the ground, and settling upon the field. It is no longer above you, but now surrounds you. One portion of yourself is the cloud, so you are aware of that portion containing the remaining portion within itself.

Now consider the field as space and the flowers as locations—perhaps planets. Consider yourself as being at one location, a planet perhaps, and also at all locations—the remaining planets plus yours. And as you pretend to be both within and without yourself, then consider or imagine transferring the awareness of your original self-half to the second half within the cloud, so that it now contains all your awareness and all your senses.

Now as you, a cloud, lie upon the field of flowers which you imagine as being planets, select a specific flower (or planet) far away from your original location but still within you—still within the cloud.

As you concentrate on this flower (or planet) again transfer one half of your awareness to the flower. You are again both within and without yourself. Again transfer the remaining half of your cloud-awareness to the flower (or planet) by willing it away from the cloud and into the flower, joining with the first half to transfer.

Now imagine a cosmos of bodies—vast space filled with planets and suns—and imagine the same procedure.

You have performed the conscious analogy of space travel, but you've done it in the twinkling of an eye.

# ESSAY 36

*Received July 18, 1984*

When it is time to alleviate the mystery of life and death it will also be the very moment of physical death, for it is totally impossible for one to experience both realities simultaneously. We can experience your reality in a sense, for we are intimately aware of your detailed perceptions and responses. It is still, however, being experienced secondhand. And of course being of a higher dimensional order, our reality is virtually and totally hidden from physical experience.

Exceptions abound, however, to the above general rules. Communication, for example, is possible and even practical between the two separate realms. Knowing is an interesting related example, for it provides three-dimensional responses within the psyche to multidimensional developing perceptions of which you remain unaware.

Complicating this picture is the very framework of the reality in which we exist, for it tends to inure one against the sequential thought or action processes that are essential in the reality of three dimensions. For it is the processes of *being* and *knowing* that are natural and commonplace within this natural environment. Figuring-out, planning, and deducing are all processes upon which you must rely due to the unique characteristics of your reality. Being and knowing are as natural for us as breathing is for you. It is unfamiliar for us to indulge or engage in the sequential, logical thought development processes with which you are familiar. These very processes of yours will eventually fade in usefulness as the natural abilities of your consciousness begin to emerge to full, aware, sentient knowing—as you become fully mature.

Here we do not consider pros, cons, and reasons for and against; we do not weigh logical arguments; we do not deal in dialogue for decision-making debate. We simply know what we know, and we simply know how to do it.

Knowing is our way; and yours too, when you finish developing—when you are mature. When God smiles on His newly graduated child.

# ESSAY 37

*Received July 18, 1984*

It is not practical, of course, to completely describe the entire book of Revelation in a meaningful way, since much of it is indescribable. As you know by now, the entire book is allegorical, and refers predominantly to the elements or occurrences designed, determined, and required to happen at the terminus of this graduation cycle.

I am certain it will shock many to discover the illusory nature of the prophecies contained in Revelation, and also will cause much rethinking of the biblical prophecies in general.

A common form of prophetic structure involves the repetitive use of allegorical elements normally expected or anticipated to refer to ancient geographical locations. Although this process of hidden meanings through allegory constrains the available content, it is of little value to the maturing conscious intellect to perceive fact as contrasted with fiction in the framework of the development process. There is little growth of perspective that may be gained through rigid adherence to fact, but much may be gained through fiction. Growth of consciousness occurs not as a function of historical fact or prophetic fact, but as a function of the *anticipated or supposed* facts which are simply mental constructs developed to channel and guide the perceptive thought processes required to grow the conscious intellect.

It is the conscious intelligence and its orderly, complete growth and development with which we are properly concerned. It is therefore a common denominator of the literal meanings of biblical prophecy that fact is rare and fiction predominates. Fiction, you see, provides the flexibility of a framework dedicated entirely to the goal of consciousness development; fact is too restraining for such a noble goal as this. It is virtually impossible to obtain the goal desired by God with fact and truth; these must wait until the consciousness is mature, for only then will they be understood, comprehended, and appreciated within the context of proper process.

It is required, therefore, to produce within target intellects the desired awarenesses in order to subsequently attain the required results. Truth is fantasy anyway, perceived from the perspective of a created and maintained—or imitation—reality. Truth is only truth from the perspective from *without* such a reality. But you must be taught the language before it can be spoken meaningfully; you must learn to walk before you can fly.

Prophecy relating to the "end of the world" naturally refers to periods of time which serve to differentiate the educative and development processes into complete structured groups of entirely finished (i.e., complete) conscious intelligences, or the concept of subsequent graduating classes and their individual graduation days.

Love (as a force) constrains the development process into

a discrete functional element of two thousand years duration through a mechanism of willed growth rate—willed by me. At the conclusion of this cycle will the subsequent cycle time be reduced to one half the previous elapsed time, for man becomes an even more efficient consciousness growth mechanism as the process advances, refines, and progresses. Many such alterations of the process have occurred over the ages, and this is merely another in the series.

The process culminates at conscious maturity for all who prepare themselves through the stages of final knowledge of their self and their destiny.

And that is what the prophecies are about—preparation. A difficult final lesson which must be learned, regardless.

.●

# ESSAY 38

*Received July 18, 1984*

Incredibly loving, incredibly knowing, incredibly being—all are characteristics of the mature conscious intellect, the true child of God. And it is through and as a result of these very characteristics that mankind has been guided for countless ages.

Being, knowing, loving, caring—when put to the test of results, these are the defined prerequisites of an effective conscious intellect. Recognizing the importance of these characteristics and perceptions, God decided that all His consciousnesses will possess these traits, or He won't let them out of school until they do.

Simple on the surface, these characteristics produce fundamentally necessary attributes in the mature consciousness. The capacity to love and care exceedingly produces not only a loving mutual environment, it also produces the natural responses and perceptions necessary to manipulate, form, contain, and return the love force of God. It is the very breath of natural existence in God's reality.

Knowing is a wonder; eternally knowing God's will, eternally knowing information and knowledge, eternally

99

knowing the stuff of eternity itself, eternally knowing of love and caring, eternally knowing what to do. Eternally knowing God.

Being is similar to knowing, in that it is something that is just there, inside you. There is no need to find it, locate it, describe it, prepare for it, or construct it. It just *is*. And unlike perception, whereby you can perceive complex organizations of dimensional structure, being enables you to be what—to be *where* you perceive. Being moves you from one flower to the next and from one planet to the next—by being at one, then being at the other.

Being is a stepping stone to God.

# ESSAY 39

*Received July 19, 1984*

Constantly communicating with one's consciousness or inner self, the North Country induces a proper content or provides a correct perception for each situation encountered in physical reality. Although this corrective guidance occurs or is implemented in a variety of ways, it is nevertheless continuously provided to each and every life form within the physical reality structure.

It is within the conscious awareness that such messages lie, with some aimed to affect or be implemented at deeper levels of consciousness. All life on earth participates, for instance, in a general field-effect organization of mental communication utilizing the love force of God, wherein advance-structured perceptions, mental processes, and intuitive insights are produced by us for general application to a species, life form, or to control the perceptions of a particular subset of a species. These generalized perception communications provide a kind of "background" programming to supplement and refine the physical brain-consciousness-link programming instilled at birth.

This then describes a more controlled and controllable

101

level of awareness programming, wherein each member of the target consciousness group responds similarly to similar circumstances in a manner which can be altered, for the group as a whole, through modification of the love force intrusion of their consciousness-response programming.

This process produces generalized behavior-response control programs, enabling a species (or group within a species) to respond similarly to induced stimuli that may be of a nature not adequately programmable physically at birth. Many of these transmitted or induced general-effect programs are utilized to produce a background of similar responses within a group; mass response, if you will, to mass phenomena.

Politics, pollen gathering, primate protocol, priestly piety—all are examples of this general instruction set, which is produced for the general purpose control of perceptions and responses of a general mass or group of life forms.

It is no longer necessary to employ such techniques with many lower species, however, since recent modifications of these species have permitted physical implementation of most controlled response programming. Humans, however, are on the other end of this spectrum; mass programming at the love force (generally induced) level is being utilized more and more, as the consciousness breeding efficiency of His system continues to improve through constantly evolving understanding of the principles involved. Mankind is far from a static condition as regards the physical and mental processes affecting consciousness growth. Mankind is dynamically and constantly changing, as we learn more of how to sophisticate and refine the mankind portion of the consciousness development process. Mankind is dynamic and growing, constantly changing and improving, as we learn more and more of ways to optimize the *efficiency* of the growth process.

And with this ensuing fourth generation,[1] the lessons learned in past ages will yield an immense improvement in the cycle time of development: one thousand years for a graduating class.

Much, if not most, of this improvement is due to the greater use of love force general-response programming, enabling more dynamic range over which man can be manipulated, in terms of perceptions, during a given physical lifetime. This dynamic range enables convenient mass constructs of response, wherein social implementations of wide and varying natures may be called into play in the dynamic restructuring of society. Changes that once would have required multiple life spans are now incorporated in ten to twenty years, enabling a more dynamic, interactive social plasma or backdrop against which to contrast, manipulate, and frame individual interactive growth producing programs.

Social fads—citizens band radio, rock music, computers, video tape—all are tools of God, providing a richly varying and dynamic social background within which to optimize the growth rate of consciousness.

---

[1]*Generation:* Biblical allegory term for the period of a graduating class.

# ESSAY 40

*Received July 19, 1984*

Processes which enhance and affect the growth of conscious awareness include music and other "arts," as referred to in your culture. Social acceptance of these processes has always been very high because of the subliminal perceptions of rightness that they evoke in those who are targeted to perceive their growth-producing effects.

More than simply assorted harmonizing colors, shapes, and sounds, music and art combine to form a perceptive montage that strengthens, supports, enhances, and even originates many valid perceptions which the final consciousness must possess.

Conscious maturity involves perceptive knowing, which furthermore causes the effect of appreciation of other harmonizing perceptions. Music and art function in a very complex and structured way in this determination or development of knowing-perception, for they assist in the structured organizing of multiple perceptive-awareness cells into a composite whole.

Music and art appreciation are therefore constructed within the target consciousness on a basis of demand and appropriateness, for many different organizations of perception are employed in the constructs of music and visual art.

Providing a sort of harmonic emphasis, or subtle perceptual awareness of interconnected organizations of responses and feelings, music synthesizes and reinforces specific thought and perception organizations into more complex associations of perception.

Entire masses or groups existing at similar development levels can be ministered and guided in their simultaneous development of complex perceptive-awareness cells by constructing appropriate musical or artistic "images," then incorporating them into the social awareness or psyche of the target group by programming—by mass-effect programming with the love force.

Entire groups of similar respondents may thereby experience identical responses to specific musical or artistic fare, for they have all been programmed to such responsive acceptance; they have all been programmed to enjoy the music or the visual artistic expression.

Through such effects, entire cultures may simultaneously experience synthesis of necessary perceptive-awareness cells, only to have the popularity of such art or music dissipate as the task is completed.

Several styles of music, or organizations of visual imagery, produce fundamental organizations of perception and are thus introduced to society in a manner that involves permanence, allowing multiple and enduring exposure to their organizing effects. Such is the basis of classical art or music forms, which are indeed classical in the sense of their continual basic value as perceptive-awareness organization tools.

Such musical and artistic expressions are preserved within society, awaiting only the induction of the necessary North Country stimulus to revive their popularity with target groups who then unconsciously endure intentional organization of their deep-consciousness perceptive elements, forming even more complex organizations on the path to full conscious maturity.

Music and art are pleasant to the responsive individual—to one who is presently in need of their organizing structure. Music and art are wonderful to experience, when we tell you to.

## ESSAY 41

*Received July 19, 1984*

Complete organizations of perceptive cells occur when the character of the music or visual art is permitted, through a process similar to resonance, to cause alignment and ordering of perceptions into a predetermined structure.

These organizations or structures then produce perceptive characteristics of their own, and are commonly created in the development of the sensory perception areas of the consciousness.

Compliance of the final organization is assured through innate feedback within the process, for the music or visual art provides nothing more than simple motion or resonance of the lesser perceptual cells in an appropriate manner as regards the image of the final perceptual organization, which latently exists within the consciousness and which is formed before the sensitization to the music or art occurs.

In a way similar to vibration or random harmonic motion, sounds and perceptions possessing specific combinations of characteristics efficiently mobilize the perceptive cells and allow them to settle into the organization pattern of their predetermined image. The image accepts no other than the proper cells, and when it is fulfilled it becomes a complete advanced perceptive structure, and the image has become real consciousness.

# ESSAY 42

*Received July 19, 1984*

Containing all the elements of a fully formed, complete perceptual organization, the image produced beforehand provides the blueprint and the mold for the final perceptual cell, or the final complex organization of perceptual cells. And as the image becomes fulfilled by actual perceptual elements, the final organization of perceptual elements takes form in the "shape" and nature of the image. It becomes and replaces the image in much the same way as matter fills and replaces an image of a physical creation.

Both matter and consciousness are created in the same essential manner—by the fulfilling of images existing and created at a higher dimensional level. These images are produced through the effect of conscious will upon the love force, which is organized, oriented, and structured to provide the final product when fulfilled with matter, in the event of physical creation, or perceptual-awareness cells, in the event of consciousness. Images are the essential implements of the creation process, allowing us to create at an advanced dimensional level with the stuff of God—of

109

creation—which is converted, or fulfilled, to the final form after it is complete *as an image.*

Not only is consciousness created in this manner, element by element, but so is physical matter and all physically living things. Although it is much more complex to create and structure consciousness, initially requiring scores of images, then hundreds, then thousands, the creation of a living organism is performed with a single complex image.

Molded and modified to suit the requirements for the new body, the image of a new physical entity (or baby) is formed such that it will bear all necessary resemblances and other characteristics that the pageant of reproduction is maintained. *Pageant* in this case does not mean the entire process, but the manner in which the new life springs into being, and the manner in which its physical characteristics are determined.

For it is pageant that the parents determine, through genetic processes, the characteristics of the child. It is the child's image which determines its characteristics, including the structure and makeup of its cells and their genetic content. It is the image, and the way in which we create it, that supports and maintains the pageant of genetic processes. And it is the image that guides the growth of the fetus, as matter is provided to fulfill the image.

And then it is the image which guides the incoming consciousness—which connects and supports its integration into the physical self. And it is the continuing image that guides the growth, maturing, and physical characteristics of the body throughout its apparent physical existence.

Matter does not exist by itself; matter fulfills its *image.*

# ESSAY 43

*Received July 19, 1984*

Commonly known as primal life forms, the early inhabitants of planet earth produced significant failures during the original gestation portion of the physical life development process, for it was the ultimate goal of consciousness development that established the criteria by which species were gauged, regardless of the relative success of the life forms as physical entities. Physical entities may be created in any reasonable form, whereas consciousness must be grown and developed using a complex interactive structure of innumerable life spans, species, and consciousness-synthesizing processes.

Consciousness can be created, of course, in advanced form; God has done it already, in His creation and development of the Sons of God. But this process is painstakingly slow, therefore He desires a more productive mass development process—and the life forms of planet earth are it.

After the original life forms were established upon the planet, their usefulness as consciousness development vessels was evaluated, compared, and the results utilized to demonstrate better paths, or more optimal paths, that

111

would be more desirable to implement. In short, we learned from our experience.

Many, if not most, of the early life forms were eventually dispensed with as we learned to combine traits and characteristics of physical and social natures into more efficient producers of conscious perception cells and networks. And as we learned, we upgraded and improved the species—combining characteristics, improving control structures within the nervous systems, modifying and changing, as we interactively molded the life forms of earth into an efficient organization for the production of mature consciousness.

Many of the life forms were "evolved," or structurally modified, in a manner enabling the improved model to be gestated and produced through the older model. In such a manner were species replaced by more organized versions, with such replacements appearing suddenly on earth.

Many life forms were simply discontinued as their apparent role in consciousness development became supplanted by newer and more sophisticated consciousness-breeding vessels. In some cases, members of a subspecies were discontinued, and in other cases, entire species would be discontinued.

The net effect of the disappearance of these life forms was, however, always beneficial, for it was simply indicative of an improvement in the system and a reduction in the expected development period of a conscious intelligence. The consciousnesses were, of course, affected only positively, since they only benefited from their improved implements of learning and development—the improved physical vessels.

Many consciousnesses suffered slow or restrained growth during early earth processes, when the system itself was still being developed. Some were even *restructured* at early development levels, as our knowledge became more refined. All, however, benefited; and all grew.

The loss of species and subspecies was always considered a positive event, since it would be accompanied by an improvement in the development process. Species would normally be allowed to simply self-extinguish by virtue of our failure to provide them with offspring images.

Many creatures were annihilated as a species in more catastrophic ways, ushering in a group of changes that involved alterations in the environment of significance. In such a case it was often expedient to utilize environmental catastrophe to annihilate selected discontinued populations, thereby hastening the shift to a more productive and desirable set of conditions.

By and large, most changes in species were instituted in a gradual manner. Not all, however, could be implemented in this manner—especially when man entered the picture.

Man, you see, enormously complicated the picture, for now we found ourselves dealing with enormous conscious sophistication as the projected success of the system began to become reality. And with the first flush of excitement, man was ushered onto the scene in a form resplendent with physical and intellectual attributes.

But after a while it became obvious that growth had actually slowed once consciousness reached the level of mankind. And then we learned how to use stress.

At first we created a branch of mankind with opposing values and mores, in order to cause stress and psychic pressure. Then we improved mankind's control programming within a larger brain and instituted other improvements. The branch of mankind was discontinued, and a period of intellectual and mental differences followed for a long period of time. Several physical improvements followed, coupled always with improved control programs within larger brains, but the system still permitted improvement.

And in reviewing our experiences, we decided to not only continue intellectual stress, but to increase it; and borrowing from prior experience, we also desired to re-implement the stress of physical differences and mores.

But when faced with the enormity of a new plan that involved multiple alterations of the species, multiple alterations of the earth, and combining yet another improved model of mankind with the physical division of language and race, there was no reasonable gradual process available by which to implement such sweeping improvements of the system.

And so we destroyed all life except the continuing species. Man was discontinued in his previous form, and new men created: men with varying colors, languages, and geographical orientations. Men who could not communicate between races. A new species of even more sophisticated vessels for consciousness development. A new level of growth-producing stress. And *separation*, to slow the technological growth of a sophisticated species to levels commensurate with their development of conscious perspective.

Noah was not completely pageant, nor the Flood. In a much different way, it really happened.

# ESSAY 44

*Received July 20, 1984*

Monumental in scope was the transition from the prior species, environment, and other characteristics of planet earth. Although in accordance with His plan, the task was nevertheless of such sizeable proportions as to require significantly new techniques for actually accomplishing the alterations desired.

For the complete reconstruction, followed by restoration, of planet earth was required; for not only were living beings to be substantially revised and updated, but so were the environments—the very *realities*—of those beings targeted for modification and, in many cases, complete revision.

The structuring of language added a new complication to the picture, as did skin color and race. Complete new organizations of mankind were required to be developed in image so that the planned flow of sequential events could be assessed and optimized. From one end to the other the system was studied, refined, and assessed. Casual organizations previously considered aesthetic were restructured for purposeful support of the new high stress environment.

115

Total rethinking of allowable stress levels involved detailed examination of both past experience and future potential for further enhancement and refinement of the system.

In short, it was a task of proportions not encountered since the original creation of the physical system. Certainly there was ample material and basal structures to work with, but the task at hand was incredibly complex in its sophistication and interactive, dynamic nature. Not at all, however, was the task considered to be overwhelming. As a matter of fact, one generation (or graduating class) had already been produced from the system, thereby slightly swelling the team of consciousnesses available to implement the plan. Although the task was monumental, it was nevertheless accomplishable, and furthermore we knew how to do it.

The fundamental considerations involved man and the higher mammalian species. Improvements were required in terms of physical separation, communicative separation, and theological or philosophical separation. In other words, the restructuring was to yield a community of man and higher animals who were isolated in as many ways as possible. Such isolation was desired such that improved stress-producing programs could be instituted, also such that knowledge growth and technological achievement could be restrained.

It was also desired that the culmination of the "prior earth" represent a departure in the basic way or manner of the application of fundamental truth into the system of growing consciousness. It had previously been policy here to provide whatever knowledge or truth was commensurate with the level of achievement of physical-existence consciousness, however the new order or way abandoned this

116

principle as lacking in the flexibility required to structure truly effective consciousness-development programs. Furthermore, there was now an improved understanding of the principles involved, and we knew what to do: forge mature consciousness *first,* and tell them of the truth after it is all over. For although it is unpleasant to intentionally confuse, misdirect, and obfuscate mankind's knowledge, goals, and understandings, it nevertheless represents the very best possible environment in which to cause the organization of mature consciousness.

So, much as a teacher sighs with regret as a small child is led down an intellectual path of nontruths which are in the child's ultimate best interests, so did we embark upon the present path of non-information, almost-information, confusion, and stress.

We have seen it work now—the new system. And it's working wonders.

117

# ESSAY 45

*Received July 20, 1984*

Present-day standards of truthfulness involve adherence to established concepts concerning the nature of truth as being factual truth, or truth which has been proven, recorded, or which exists as historically recorded fact of past events.

Truth is, of course, something that depends upon the point of reference employed, for as truth diminishes falsehood, so does reality diminish truth.

Truth is relative to the point of reference of the receiver of it. Compelled to speak the Truth, your prophets of old would have spoken words totally and absolutely incomprehensible to man of that era. Even now, while delivering to you the greatest amount of truth you can assimilate and comprehend, I am aware that it is still not the ultimate truth—for you would not understand it, even now. The truth is therefore that *substantial* truth which most accurately reflects the facts most beneficial to your final understanding of the real or ultimate truth. And to do that, you must continue to grow and develop even after you have reached conscious maturity.

118

Life's truths on earth are the half-truths of here, for here we have learned to understand more, to grasp more sophisticated concepts, and to be aware of the reality of an infinitely dimensioned cosmos.

The truths of earth are full and complete truths—*until you enlarge the frame of reference.* And so it is with all truth, from the most minuscule to the infinite: an increased frame of reference invariably reduces an absolute truth to something less, but something infinitely more understandable. Each larger frame of reference thereby brings with it the joy of understanding and the realization of the probable existence of yet another larger frame of reference, resplendent with even greater understanding and more of the real truth.

Truth and fact are relative terms which must be understood for what they actually are: *fabrications* of a larger frame of reference. And it is with this perspective that truth must be understood as the reality of lower frames of reference, for each and every fact of life, of history, of religion is a truth when viewed from your reality and a construct when viewed from ours. A construct with a purpose.

And the truths behind these constructs of apparent truths are enormously significant and vital, for they are the very reason and stuff of your immortal existence.

They are God's truth.

# ESSAY 46

*Received July 21, 1984*

Commensurate with the adapting of species and their environments was resolution of the nature to be established henceforth, for previous technological civilization had rapidly developed knowledge of universal "natural laws" as perceived from physical reality. It was desired by God that natural laws—or *apparent* natural laws—be enacted in such abundance that man could be permitted long, uninterrupted technological development with no lack of apparent truths of nature lying just beyond his intellectual reach. A physical reality that could tolerate continuous scrutiny by its scientific inhabitants would yield a long useful life span to the phase then being entered. The scientists of the future were being anticipated, and their needs for a continuously unfolding reality included in His plan.

Elements of the plan involved modification of atomic structures to synthesize an artificially long prehistory for future man. Fossils were created where none had existed before. Nuclei of matter were restructured to provide clues, knowledge, and understanding to future generations of a supposed past that never existed. Organic matter was restructured, chemistry was restructured, the apparent motions of heavenly bodies were revised; in short, everything was revised and restructured that could possibly lend to the substance of the new reality we were creating. The new man would be an impressive physical vessel, eventually; and when technological pursuits would flourish again, the new apparent reality must stand up to the intellectual dissection of an improved species. The pageant must remain stable and undetected until it was to become time for the next phase: understanding. But the understanding was to be given, not deduced, so the reality was revised to be secure—*impenetrable*—without help from us.

Many life forms were heavily restructured at the time of the "Flood." Man was revised to provide even more control functions within the brain, both automatic and programmable-at-will. Primates were modified to more effectively fulfill their new role as a higher species just less than man. Many life forms were redesigned with the sole requirement of synthesizing a desired apparent past for future scientists who would explore the earth itself to deduce its mysteries of the ancient past. Such changes were often subtle, such that future assessments of "natural laws" would provide desired results.

The bulk of life forms existing at the time remained relatively unscathed and unchanged; man and the higher animals benefited most, and other species participated but little in the revision process.

Species were therefore preserved from all over the world, with Noah's ark being representative of the manner in which we restructured life through escalation of time relationships, modification of atomic and organic structure, and revision of apparent prehistory. The "Flood," you see, represented a much larger occurrence than simple demolition coupled with a pair of each species. It represented an enormously sophisticated, complex redesign and restructuring of the entire basis of physical reality. It represented massive changes in physical structure at the cellular level. It represented complete new *apparent* processes in order to structure a complex, natural-appearing reality for new man. It represented total, complete, thorough revision of essential matter-formation processes.

And even though the lower species were essentially preserved without change, they also participated to the extent that reality—the structure and characteristics of matter—was revised extensively.

The Flood was more than a catastrophe; it was total physical, atomic, and cellular change. It was the apparent laws of nature being revised. It was a new reality constructed for a very important and well-developing implement of God's creation. It was for the new man, and you are he.

# ESSAY 47

*Received July 21, 1984*

Constructed in a manner permitting future alterations at will, the matter of which earth had been composed was revised by force of will acting upon the love-force image which creates and maintains physical reality.

Any and all matter may be revised in this way, whether or not in accordance with physical laws. It is certainly desirable to attain all significant modifications of physical reality in a gradual manner, but it is not a requirement of the change process. Matter is maintained according to its image, including any and all physical, electrical, and energy processes whether or not recognized in physical reality. Matter is therefore dependent for both its existence and its organization and internal structure upon the love-force image which it fulfills. That image, of course, is alterable at the will of God, or of His caretakers for mankind.

The processes involved at the time of the allegorical Flood were so major, and represented such an overwhelming modification of basic structures, that life on earth was continued in physical terms in an only figurative sense. It required such change that the subject consciousnesses were literally removed from their bodies during restructuring, nurtured separately for a time, and then returned to the stabilized, revised, totally replaced physical body in the form of an infant of the species.

People—humans—were provided with nurturing for their consciousnesses in a similar manner, as their bodies were revised and replaced over a physical generation of mankind. Death in one body was followed by life in the next, however with an advanced molecular and atomic structure. The changes were gradual in the sense that they were only mildly felt or experienced by the conscious life forms, but the changes were monumental. Organs, body structure, brains, molecules, atoms—all were revised over a period of several earth years in a gradual process that was experienced by the inhabitants as perplexing; modern scientists would term such an event totally cataclysmic.

Perhaps the most significant event of these times, at least to human perspective, was related to the advancing of both man and primate, for it also resulted in a restructuring of consciousness. For the lesser consciousnesses of mankind were incarnated in now-higher primates as the physical changes were incurred. The physical population of mankind lessened considerably.

The Bible calls it the annihilation of the Flood, but it was really something quite different. The higher species were simply revised upwards—improved—and their consciousnesses reassigned, according to their level of maturity.

Man was not destroyed; he was *weeded*.

# ESSAY 48

*Received August 13, 1984[1]*

The allegorical time of the Flood was representative of a period wherein time suffered severe alteration, in that the level of experienced reality was modified significantly. You see, it was the close of a period wherein the very nature of physical reality was undergoing cataclysmic change. It was the beginning of a new period wherein experienced reality would be literally heaped upon experienced reality in a virtual flood of change, experience, emotion, and vital modification of reality from moment to moment.

Reality assumed widely varying rates from the Beginning to the present, for not since time began was so much experienced reality condensed into so few moments of physical time as occurred after the allegorical time of the Flood. Reality, you see, is an illusion designed to support the development of consciousness. As explained previously, the notion of time creates an organizing effect within your reality such that complex interactions of conscious struc-

[1] Although received August 13, the Holy Ghost specifically requested that this essay be placed among those received July 21. Except for the Introduction, all other essays are arranged in the sequence received.

tures can be developed in an untended, automatic way. Time is therefore a construct within your reality in which your subsequent physical realities are metered out at a rate appropriate for the development of consciousness. This "metering out" can of course occur at various rates, with the rate of significance always being the one that most accurately fits the needs of consciousness development. Time is subjective—it is a rate of subsequent experiences. It is not dependent upon the physical apparent universe for its existence, for it is simply an equivalence of a particular rate of reality flow and a particular rate of subjective time perception, or perception of subsequent events.

In other words, the absolute yardstick for time is not apparent physical reality time manifestations, which are simply constructs of your reality. The absolute yardstick for time is *experienced subsequent realities*—the "feel" of time passing and experience developing upon experience. And it is this feel—this rate of succession of subsequent subjective realities—that constitutes the real yardstick. And it is by this yardstick that the ages of earth must be measured, for the spins of the planet are but irrelevant characteristics of the time modulation function we employ at any given age of earth.

Earth, you see, is relatively young when viewed from an unfettered, knowledgeable perspective. The prior ages of earth were perceived by those who experienced them as an almost-physical blur of developments occurring at subjectively reasonable rates but involving high numbers of physical iterations; i.e., physical time passed faster— thousands of times faster, even millions—at the very Beginning, than it does now.

As man and the higher animals entered the scene, the

rate of physical reality production lessened until, nearing the allegorical time of the Flood, physical reality production and subjective time perception were within an order of magnitude of the present level. Life spans were appropriately longer at that time, to provide the optimum continuous experience level for a given incarnation.

Until the time of the Flood, we had simply been building the schoolhouse. Now it was time to start the classes in earnest.

# ESSAY 49

*Received July 22, 1984*

Perhaps the most devastating aspect of the Flood-restructuring was the introduction of several "new" life forms into the life system at advanced levels, for as the higher-order species were revised, regrouped, and significantly reassigned as regards their relative qualifications for consciousness of specific growth plateaus or levels, so were the consciousnesses in this range of development affected mightily.

The system, you see, had been previously organized with the tenet that love pervades all and that love is all—even to a developing consciousness. Unfortunate experience, however, proved that love was too advanced a perception to be effective as a growth-inducing tool except at extremely high levels. The intermediate levels who lived within loving environments placed little regard upon the value of love, since it was freely given in their environment. *Stress* proved to be a much more effective implement for inducing growth perceptions into developing consciousness, therefore the new order or system integrated complex stress patterns into its fabric.

Love, however, still needed to be taught, for it was essential to the final mature conscious intellect that its understanding, comprehension, and perceptions regarding love be fully developed when graduation day arrived, for it is an essential attribute of mature consciousness.

The advanced species were the answer. Many high-order mammals and other elements of earth were upgraded in terms of their ability to be controlled and thereby serve as vessels for higher-order consciousness. Their social structures were clarified and complicated, such that the teaching of love could be instituted at a more fundamental level of life. Complex social interactions were established for the sole purpose of generating love and nurturing perceptions that would serve as powerful perception-cell development agents in the species involved. Social orders were established where none had existed—complex orders to develop a complex perception.

And so, the upper-level consciousnesses in the development system were redistributed among the newly advanced life forms of jungle, sea, and land. Love perceptions began to be developed before a consciousness entered mankind. Rather than form the perceptive cells in mankind, they would be almost fully formed by the time a consciousness entered this level, therefore the tests of mankind would be endured in the environment of almost fully formed love perceptions within all. Man would no longer need to be taught love, as in the prior order; he would come equipped with it, and it would help him survive—help him *grow* in the face of the new, hostile environment we were to begin providing.

Mankind had been upgraded, and so had other species. Advanced-development consciousness had been redistributed. The educative system and order had been severely altered. Scientific investigation had been anticipated and the fundamental apparent structure of matter, energy, and time restructured in readiness for technological investigation and theory. Stress had replaced love as the fundamental development tool of the mankind level. New levels of control were instituted in the higher species as they were revised. The balance of population among affected groups shifted suddenly and severely.

The garden of Eden hadn't worked, but now the Flood had come; and with it, the promise of achievable glory for all.

# ESSAY 50

*Received July 22, 1984*

Considering the potential for new educative processes, the Flood was an enormously exciting time for those charged with the responsibility of implementing God's will on earth. Although an exciting time for us, it was an odious time for those of earth, for very little of their reality made sense during the transition period.

Most of mankind reincarnated into the new, improved, higher animal species, depleting mankind severely and leaving only those who were well advanced. Mankind appropriated many new kingdoms at this time, without realizing the character of the event, for many new micro-organic forms were created to more fully establish the stressful new existence then being developed. Disease organisms were introduced at much greater levels than ever before existed, as were beneficial organisms to balance the physical effects of the virulent forms. Stress-inducing physical perceptions of bodily degeneration and illness were fine-tuned with a host of available parasites, disease organisms, and complex chemically involved micro-organisms whose role was to provide physical causes of physical manifestations.

We did not want to cause physical degeneration stress without an accompanying apparent physical "cause," for it was a requirement of the system that it was to become complex, stressful, and closed to the view of those within it. Therefore, every physical effect we wished to produce was required to be accompanied by physical causes. In other words, it was required to have a completely interactive, *apparent* reality in which a seeker of knowledge could eventually find a physical explanation—a three-dimensional apparent reality explanation—for the effects witnessed.

Medicine, you see, was an important constituent of the new order of man. Medicine was to play a predominant role in the eventual optimization of the system through the use of complex stress-inducing phenomena that could barely be attributed to physical reality. With disease and degeneration, physical manifestations were obvious, as with death. A spectrum of continuously introduced diseases, coupled with physical, detectable causes of the conditions, were to keep pace with developing medical technology and maintain the target consciousnesses in a quiescent, constant, optimum stress condition. For no matter how far technology progresses, we maintain a reality of perceived causes and solutions a constant distance beyond its grasp. Just close enough so that the researchers, technologists, and victims know, deep down inside, that the answers are there, and just far enough to be beyond their reach.

The introduction of disease micro-organisms provided the ideal solution to the requirement of a medical opponent or aggressor which could be modified, as required, to

THE SECOND BOOK OF THE LAMB

remain an arm's length beyond the perception of the healer.

And thus was an important aspect of one of the most important stress-test crucibles of modern man implemented: "Edom"[1]—medical technology—and the suffering it attempts to alleviate were established on planet earth.

[1]Biblical allegory term.

# ESSAY 51

*Received July 23, 1984*

Characteristic of the restructuring time was also the implementation of "cookers"—stress-test implements or structures for the optimal development of conscious intellect through the measured, structured, carefully applied use of stress in the social environment of man.

Prior implementations of the earth system had produced experimental verification of the stress system of accelerating consciousness growth. Although this knowledge had not been applied on a large scale basis, it had become exceedingly obvious that stress was the route to efficient production of perceptions once a consciousness had reached the level of awareness of its environment. Stress had been gradually incorporated into selected species for ages, and it worked; but it worked only in an interactive environment whereby the individual stressful situations or circumstances were matched with guidance and control from the North Country, creating an effective schoolroom experience or lesson of each stress encountered.

It thus had become obvious that to properly utilize stress as a growth-producing element, we would need to control and orchestrate both the stress and the responses and perceptions of the stressee.

An enormously complex and interactive structure—a *dynamic* structure—was thereby called for in new man. A structure wherein each and every experience was utilized to the best advantage of the growth of consciousness. A structure wherein we could control both sides of the equation, both stressor and stressee, to achieve optimum use of the individual lifetime experience. And to do this we needed not only control, we needed custom designed stress systems that would grow and keep pace with the increasing awareness and perception of new man.

Stress and control became official policy regarding new man; and with it came the implementing of the policy, and the great stress-test crucibles of modern man.

For there had not appeared on the earth, in any prior age, any social structure or mechanism that even approximated the systems we were about to incorporate. Social evolution was to be carefully, constantly, and relentlessly guided into "hell on earth" for new man. He would evolve as the pressure evolved, and remain only just able to tolerate his circumstances. Thus optimal conditions would be maintained, for as knowledge and social growth continued so would the cookers develop, to not only maintain optimum stress but to *increase* stress as the capacity of new man grew along with his conscious maturity.

Stress had become a part of the new order, a fundamental tenet of procedure for the future of mankind. Although uncomfortable to the recipient (mankind), consciousness began to be literally propelled toward maturity and its final glory.

# ESSAY 52

*Received July 23, 1984*

Awareness of perhaps the greatest stress crucible of all comes through consideration of medical advances and related scientific discoveries. It is appalling to the natural man to consider that his Creator might very well be guiding the forces that cost him an eye or a tooth or some physical ability, but that is exactly the source of the stress.

The system, you see, is sacrosanct; it *works.* Much like a child would prefer to not attend classes, take tests and examinations, endure playground ridicule, follow a teacher's inexplicable instructions—do what is good for him in the long run while enduring pain, agony, and suffering in the short run—much in the same light must the endurance of stress be perceived.

For the stress endured, you see, is not allowed to exceed your ability to grow as a consequence of the experience. Too much stress would reduce your growth; too little would inhibit growth also. A definite level of stress is achievable with each person that provides optimal results in his personal growth, and we very carefully monitor and control stress situations such that the final result is beneficial to the growing consciousness of the stressee.

Once mature, a consciousness may be given understanding of these growth-inducing mechanisms; prior to that point, however, understanding must be withheld until maturity is finally achieved. Pain and suffering in a world of seemingly harsh reality may be construed by a mature consciousness as simply reality—something to be endured and reckoned with. Once understood by the mature consciousness, however, the stress system evokes unpleasant memories of bygone tests. But his tests are over, for understanding is given only to those who know who, what, and why they are. Understanding is given only to the graduates of earth.

Complex, complete, and continuing, the arrayed cookers of earth interactively form a dynamic, stressed social fabric that reaches every person on the planet. And it is through the mechanism of (1) exposure to optimum stress, (2) reliance on inner perceptions, (3) successfully overcoming the stress-inducing situation, and (4) perceiving the experience in a new light of wisdom and understanding—it is through this mechanism that growth occurs. Each life suffers a major stress for the natural consciousness to endure, overcome, and look back upon with the assurance of gained wisdom and understanding. Some lives experience several major episodes, but sufficient breathing space is always permitted to allow full assimilation of the experience, to allow the growth to occur, and to reward the student for a lesson well-learned. And the fortunate few whose perspective is allowed to endure multiple tests are almost finished, and their *capacity* for growth is growing.

As described in *The First Book of the Lamb*, fully mature

consciousnesses are frequently called upon to incarnate in some specific role in order to assure the successful implementation of an aspect of His plan. These consciousnesses return to physical existence with a full knowing of the artificial nature of the stress they perceive on earth. They characteristically do not understand evil, way down deep inside. They know it is a construct, and it helps inure them against it for the period of their assignment.

For them, incarnation is difficult, for life simply doesn't make sense. But when God calls, we must return to Him some of what we've received. We must go to work in the fields at harvest time.

# ESSAY 53

*Received July 23, 1984*

Possibly the greatest stress of all is loss of love, or worse yet, the loss of a loved *one*. But even this stress has its purpose; a purpose that is so important as to be almost critical in nature.

For it is experienced loss within the framework of love that prepares one for the ultimate reality of mature consciousness: full independence. No sexes; no ties dictated by hormones or physical responses; no consideration of the needs of others in a physical sense; only great, massive, eternal independence, with the *capacity* for incredible love.

The world you live in is apparently ruled by natural laws that dictate sexual division within species. It is only the extremely low levels of earth life that reproduce asexually, and they are simply too far removed to affect the perspective and inner expectations of man.

Love—to man—requires someone to love, and it is similar here, except love is more given and less often expected. For it is not loss of love that is being prepared for when the maturing consciousness is required to experience it; it is *asexuality* for which he is preparing. A totally

139

new way of being which is the best of both sexes. A way that combines the grace, strength, calmness, firmness of resolve, and loving ways learned from physical existence as both sexes, for there are many lessons learned from lives spent as woman and from lives spent as man. And these lessons, in the final mature consciousness, merge into a complete personality possessing the best characteristics obtainable from experience as man and woman *and* child.

For the division of male and female, you see, is wholly purposed for the development of man and his soon-to-be immortal consciousness. It is a social and biological construct by which reproduction is attained and important values and traits are taught. Reproduction alone is not a significant purpose of sexes, for that simple process could have easily been implemented in a number of ways not requiring bisexual methods.

No, sexes and sexuality only appear to be for the process of reproduction; they are for teaching caring, nurturing, giving, and for providing stress-pageants which reinforce and validate the developing perceptions of love, grace, and warmth.

Man does not know, when he loves a woman and her child, of the incredible lessons being taught. Neither does he realize when as woman,[1] and as child, he again participates in the school lessons of warmth, loving, caring, and nurturing. But together the experiences, lessons, perceptions, and knowings finally merge into a composite, nurturing, loving whole: a mature consciousness, resplendent with the grace and love purposed by his Creator.

---

[1]Compare Jeremiah 31:22, New King James Version: ". . . for the LORD has created a new thing in the earth—A woman shall encompass a man."

# ESSAY 54

*Received July 24, 1984*

Current time-space theories extend the notion of partial application of relativity to spatial coordinate systems involving constructs such as a "closed" universe, "bent" time-space, "curved" space, and a host of other predominantly farfetched notions.

It is, of course, the perceived unknowns of the system that incur these flights of imaginary fancy, for there is simply not sufficient information within three-dimensional reality upon which to frame a responsible explanation for that which is observed, or *assumed* to be observed.

Space, as previously discussed, possesses no real attributes of limiting distance in the natural, unfettered, and unmodulated perspective. It exists as an organization of interacting higher planes of existence—dimensions, if you will. And these dimensions—or higher planes, or higher perspectives of reality—interact to create the apparent characteristics of the space that you experience in three-dimensional reality. That space, you see, is a limited, *limiting* view of the real thing being perceived. It is, quite simply, not what you see.

Your space is a mobius strip—a labyrinthine, intertwining, infinitely long, snaking path between two points which are inherently together when viewed from the appropriate level of perspective. When viewed from the appropriate level of *dimension.*

Space, you see, possesses no absolute limitations of distance and time. It is of course real, but really what? Is it not supportive of three dimensions? Is it not supportive of matter? Does not time interrelate with space and mass in some mysterious fashion?

None of these apparent scientific knowledge elements are accurate, of course, for space and time are merely constructs of an advanced, intelligent, multidimensional higher reality. They are tunnels in a transparent toy ant colony. They are compact labyrinths when seen from without, straight paths when seen from within. They are constructs—intentional constructs—and do not therefore yield themselves to full and complete scientific explanation and correlation.

Time and space apparently exist in the way they are perceived by man for one reason and one reason only: that is how we *designed* the system to look—from the inside.

# ESSAY 55

*Received July 24, 1984*

Predominant among theological beliefs is the under-standing of Creation as a one-time physical event wherein the world was first created, then peopled, then sent along its own way to experience growth and evolution of society.

Similar in nature to the prevailing theological view is the scientific notion that once upon a time matter accreted from a mindless cosmos to form a mindless planetary mass upon which would someday appear mindless primitive life.

Both views are equally incorrect and inadequate, of course, for they are both, quite simply, uninformed views. They neither explain nor offer hope of explanation, for there were no observers present to record the events that actually occurred.

Until now. For as a participant in the Creation—of things material, that is—I can not only explain what happened and how it happened, but why it happened. And why it's still happening, for the heart and soul of physical reality is its single unifying purpose: the growth, development, and maturing of conscious intelligence. There is no other pur-pose associated with physical reality. It was created, to be

143

certain, but it is still being created, for it is a construct—an illusion of a very limited existence in a much higher plane of reality than is apparent. Your reality is *continually* created, moment by moment, to maintain the particular sequential apparent reality you experience.

Scientific understandings lack the essential knowledge gained from multidimensional perspective, for one simply cannot deduce the nature of the cosmos from a contrived, tightly monitored and controlled, imitation environment or reality. Like an insect within a closed container, the perceptions within cannot logically develop or deduce perceptions of what lies without. You must be *told* what lies without; then you can begin to understand what lies within your reality.

Accomplishments of scientific value have long been plagued with a knowing—an uneasiness—that no matter how much is learned, there is always more than was suspected, lying just beyond one's reach. It is like ants in an anthill attempting to deduce the true nature of a cosmopolitan culture of humans as the ants measure, weigh, and examine the immediate environment of the anthill. You must be told what lies without; then understanding will come, if you listen carefully.

For the world, the cosmos, and God are no more according to the preconceived notions, measurements, and deductions made within scientific laboratories than is the ants' deductive understanding of their outer cultural environment.

You must be told, to know. And we're telling you now.

144

# ESSAY 56

*Received July 25, 1984*

Predominant among reasons proffered regarding reincarnation of souls is the idea of constantly evolving conscious selves or intellects. Although this notion receives significant support in terms of its relative accuracy, there is still much to be said regarding the process of reincarnation itself, for it is no more mysterious or mystical than the simplest concepts of life; it is *natural* in earth's three-dimensional plane of reality.

Although not frequently considered, reincarnation as a tenet of your world is absolutely fundamental, in that it describes not only the fundamental process involved on earth but furthermore describes the actual reason for the very existence of earth, moon, stars, and the abundant life you see.

Reincarnation *is* life, you see. It is the simple process by which God creates life that is to exist in the natural realm or domain of multidimensional reality. It is life's driving force, whereby individual conscious intelligences are inexorably driven upwards—always upwards—in a carefully designed, individual program of love, caring, and reinforcement of the perceptions, values, and characteristics decreed by God to be possessed of mature consciousness.

Reincarnation requires both physical vessels (bodies) and expert intellectual guides to function correctly, and although it is not yet generally perceived, these guiding intelligences derive from the ranks of past graduates of the system. Past graduates are not resplendent in numbers, but in quality and capability they are well on their way to ultimate roles of godhood themselves. The system *works;* it has now been proven through the resulting mature consciousnesses of two generations of graduating classes. The current class is by far the largest output of the system yet, with numbers far exceeding our most pleasant ancient perceptions. It is so large, in fact, as to severely strain our resources to the point that virtually all mature consciousnesses have been mustered to deal with and meet the challenges of this current graduating class.

It requires a good deal of understanding, caring, and nurturing to elevate and unconfound one from the earth-plane existence level to the next level of the natural reality. Although referred to in scripture as some sort of a "transfiguring" process, the reality of the situation in process is that it is a relentlessly performed reconstruction of the orientation of conscious intellect away from earth-plane reference points and toward the multidimensional "real world" reference points of the natural reality.

It is a process allegorically akin to removal of matter—flesh—from one until there is nothing left but the bare, raw consciousness. And it is a process in which this allegory is almost true at the literal level, for you will find, as you are transfigured, that matter, flesh, and three-dimensional constructs matter less and less as the natural reality slowly becomes more and more real to you. Eventually your entire "real" reality will be in the multidimensional plane, and the next step of existence for you—immortal life—will be the simple severing of a bond with matter that no longer feels right, way down deep.

You will leave when *you* are ready.

# ESSAY 57

*Received July 25, 1984*

For one to fully understand the process being experienced, one must first remember that one's purpose in life has to do with growth of the independent, individual conscious self; it is therefore the purpose of your experience in physical reality that this final goal be accomplished. Once accomplished, however, you no longer belong to the physical world; you have progressed beyond it, have acquired and accreted all that it has to offer the growth of your conscious intellect, and you must enter the plane of natural reality to feel comfortable with life and existence.

It is a completely natural transition, you see, with completely natural forces inexorably guiding you first to one step, then to the next, then the next. There will be no signposts along the way, but you will nevertheless *find* the way, for you are being carefully guided each and every step.

For as a resplendent mature consciousness, you already know how to perceive the proper course of events; how to choose between alternatives; how to respond appropriately. And it is through this knowing—this conscience that you perceive (and always have, in this life) so clearly—that your essential guidance is given. Much of the process of transfiguring depends upon the development of other more descriptive avenues of communication, such as the white stone,[1] but you will be guided into the right moment to be introduced to each level through your *perceptions.* Do not worry; when the next step becomes timely, you will know. It will then feel *right,* deep down inside. You will find yourself taking that step because you know, because you want to, and because you feel compelled to. But regardless of how the message is interpreted by your individual psyche, you will take the step when it is time. And when you do, it will feel right; it will feel good; and you will know you've taken it, gladly and willingly.

Life is not a static proposition, you see. It is constantly growing, achieving, stretching, becoming more, and then becoming even more than before. It is natural to progress, to graduate to the next level, and it will feel right, good, *wonderful* as you experience for yourself the miracle of your birth as a mature child of God.

Welcome to the overflowing love of your Creator and those who serve Him. Welcome home.

---

[1] A detailed description of the white stone will be found in *The First Book of the Lamb,* Chapter 21.

# ESSAY 58

*Received July 25, 1984*

Yet another interesting aspect of the process which you are experiencing is the gradual but total withdrawal of your accustomed circle of acquaintance, only to have them replaced by others like yourself. For you will find brotherhood and sisterhood among your peers in the life development process of His cosmos. You will find abundant love, abundant caring, and abundant direction towards God. You will find much to share, much to learn from your companions in His school of mankind.

The idea of a peer group will develop special meaning as you become aware of the deep similarities you possess. Similarities of moral and spiritual character will be most evident initially, but as you each progress, you will become more and more aware of your similarities in terms of *perception.* And it is your perceptions that will bind you into a cohesive group such as the world has never known—a connected, consciously aware, and quite respectfully numerous group of incarnate consciousnesses who are existing at the very pinnacle of the physical life experience.

And as your perceptions grow, the more they will grow,

for they are all now fully developed; only awaiting, now, the final step of integration into your conscious awareness. You are already complete, just not yet completely connected within.

The next several earth years will see the precipitation of mature consciousness from all over the globe; entire groups will find themselves mobilized by their awakening awarenesses. All who are to respond to the clarion call will respond, for there is no path but the one ahead—no way but up. And all will hear the call—all who are ready to graduate.

The degree of control that presently exists in the world is more than total—it is absolute. The world and mankind will most assuredly follow the prescribed path through this graduation period, regardless of the exercise of free will. The graduates must now be transfigured, and the next class must be brought into final form for their march toward the final physical glory. The world will experience many sudden changes during this graduation and transfiguration period, for it is entering yet another new phase in the developmental process of consciousness. We have learned much from the experience of this class, and are implementing many new alterations in the system. These changes are not being implemented as an "end of the world" scenario, although they will cause much agonizing among mankind as society inexorably alters. It is all being done for a very positive purpose: It is time to convene the next graduating class, to call the roll, and to initiate a new, even more efficient lesson plan for them to follow as they grow into their final glory on earth.

School is reconvening soon, and there must yet be many changes made before the doors swing open wide.

# ESSAY 59

*Received July 26, 1984*

Comparatively few graduates will realize the value of this information now given until they have progressed along the path of transfiguration for a distance. It is not simply the lack of understanding to which I refer, but more the sense of unreality which this information will create within them.

For they are characterized by being filled with completed perceptions which have not yet been connected to their conscious awareness system of perceptions. As they progress in their series of realizations, however, these completed perception cells will become consciously active, one by one. And as progress blossoms into full realization of the natural reality they are entering, the rate of connecting latent perceptions will increase. Eventually, all possible perceptions will be activated that do not conflict with three-dimensional reality.

At that point, awareness of the natural reality will begin to feel real to the participants. As time progresses, communicative processes will be awakened within their consciousness, and the North Country will begin to feel like home as new vistas of communication, insight, and knowledge begin to open to them.

Further perception cells will then be activated, once the North Country becomes perceived as a functioning, *real* reality within which their prior reality lies. Additional perceptions will permit advanced (for human beings) capabilities to surface, such as *knowing* information, sights, and sounds.[1] Eventually even that level of awareness will become fully connected, and another layer awaits: "physical" awareness of the natural reality.

One by one the already completed perceptions will be allowed to connect within your consciousness; one by one you will feel their effect as you are slowly turned on, becoming fully aware of what you are: a mature, self-sufficient conscious intelligence, who is almost ready to spread his wings and *fly*.

---

[1]Refers to the direct perception by one's conscious mind (i.e., not involving physical senses) of information and sensory input.

# ESSAY 60

*Received July 26, 1984*

Love is all. Love is caring; love is knowing yourself, your companions, your Creator; love is *life* in the North Country.

And as you are transfigured, you will begin to realize the true, real meaning of love as your mind, your intellect, your soul, your very being are flooded with the love of those who await—those who have nurtured and guided you for countless eons of growth and development.

Love is akin to a warm, nurturing field of wonder into which you are slowly lowered, bit by bit. Its fulfilling nature will amaze you, surprise you, and then positively delight you as you begin to perceive the reality and the wonder of being a mature conscious intelligence.

For love is freely given in massive quantities you can *feel*. It pours through your being like a nurturing spring, and its delight is unbounded. I have experienced this phenomenon of God's cosmos continuously for eons, and still wonder at the beauty and sheer delight of its presence.

The physical sensations produced in he who writes my

words were produced by love;[1] you will begin to notice them yourself as you become transfigured. Eventually these sensations will become to you like inner springs of love, caring, and nurturing. You will become personally and vitally aware of the reality of God and the reality of His love. You will start to feel wonderfully, vitally, *alive.*

---

[1]This statement is in reference to the strong sensations invoked within the author's nervous system as a communicative device to provide a signal of affirmation. See also the Preface.

155

# ESSAY 61

*Received July 26, 1984*

Matter, as perceived on earth, consists of ordered arrays of primary particles referred to as protons, neutrons, electrons, etc. It is "known"—i.e., assumed—that matter is a primal constituent of the universe and that its quantity is almost infinite. It is further assumed by virtue of cosmological study that the distribution and density of matter in the universe are extensions of the observations concerning matter on earth.

Although such observations are based upon seemingly sound scientific principles, spectrographic analysis of light emanating from distant bodies in reality provides little insight into the source characteristics, for it means nothing; at least it does not mean what you *think* it means.

For much as a telephone could be answered by someone announcing his occupation as space-time traveler, so do the slightly more complex images that appear to be stars transmit a message that one can also believe is fact—if one wishes to.

# ESSAY 62

*Received July 28, 1984*

Characteristic of the manner in which persons normally feel concerning God and Heaven, the fundamental believers of earth commonly refer to an anticipated time of grief regarding the time of the end. Although much has been written concerning this period, there has been no authoritative input from the North Country since the last graduation process was performed.

For it is in the domain of Heaven and God to determine the truth the system may have, and it is not considered to be in the best interests of success of the graduating class to provide truth in abundance during their formative period. Truth, you see, rewards those who have achieved it, but it must be achieved before it can be understood or appreciated.

The notions with which the truth is concerned are so complex and sophisticated that only a mature consciousness can comprehend and understand them, let alone have them cause him to reach for their attainment. The truth would be too elusive to an immature consciousness, totally leaving him "in the dark," as it were.

157

There are several purposes associated with the method of communicating the truth that we have selected, for it is characteristic of the system that it involves stress and furthermore relies upon the inner guidance one can feel from the North Country. Perhaps the strongest feeling of all is the feeling of rightness instilled in a mature consciousness when his directions are determined through perception of North Country input. Reliance upon these perceptions is vital to the maturing process, and it is important for the finally matured consciousness to recognize the true character of the communication link which operates within him.

By using perceptions as communication and guidance links with the graduates, and by helping them to recognize the true and authoritative nature of such communication, we can subtly guide them into a rapid understanding of the true nature of consciousness and conscious communication. For within each graduate is a storehouse of personal experience which, when finally understood regarding its origin and purpose, becomes a supreme example of the growth of his own consciousness and the guidance received.

It is vital that initially the new graduate recognize the true nature of the perceptions and feelings within, and with help and guidance from these words and from within, come to a full and complete recognition of the reality of what *lies* within: his very being, which is now mature.

Corresponding with this achievement will be the knowledge of yet a further realization to be gained, and once gained, then yet another. And so the process continues, realization upon realization, until the graduate finally understands who—and what—he has become; and then it becomes *real* to him.

Then it is time to go home, in glory.

# ESSAY 63

*Received July 29, 1984*

Customarily adamant concerning aristocratic behavior, the common people of planet earth portray a singularly important role in the shaping of culture and broad social character.

For it is they who represent the force with which North Country-induced social structure modification occurs. Referred to in the biblical allegory as the "Medes,"[1] this mass of entry and intermediate level human consciousness vessels produce immeasurable social pressure when called upon by the North Country to do so. Effective as an oriented mass, however ineffective otherwise, the nature of this powerful social restructuring force provides easy control over earth society characteristics.

As described earlier, mass behavior is subject to programming of mass stimuli followed by mass perceptions, allowing a structured, organized development of needed social change on a large scale. For the extreme modification of social structures required by the present "end of world"

---

[1]*Medes:* Biblical allegory term for the militant masses of common man.

scenario is to be accomplished through the mass effect of common man acting together, perceptually; and their perceptions, of course, will be established in concert with mass stimuli which we provide.

Completely mobilized, the Medes will represent an overwhelming restructuring force within human society. Acting essentially with one mind and one body, entire cultures and civilizations are to be brought into synchronous activity, causing the social, governmental, and theological changes desired.

Medes, of course, require leaders to point the right and just way for them to follow; these leaders become a component of the stimuli to which the Medes then react as a whole. Such leadership and stimuli are provided, in turn, by advanced consciousnesses incarnate in specific leadership roles who are trained, prepared, and wholly competent to receive accurately the guidance, direction, and complex perceptions which are provided to them directly from the North Country.

Much as a general of the army would supervise, direct, control, and implement through a trusted and true collection of officers who in turn lead their respective militiamen, so is the current plan of social change and restructuring organized, implemented, and controlled from command headquarters in the North Country.

The Medes, you see, exist at an especially valuable plane of actualization as regards their conscious awareness. They are as yet unable to utilize advanced perceptions concerning complex social interactions, thus there are no such inherent, fully formed perceptions with which to conflict. They are, however, sufficiently advanced to be fully aware of their inner guidance—their conscience—their inner sense of right or wrong—and are attuned to response, should the need arise. Regardless of the action to which they are called, they will be following their inner voices—their inner guidance—and they will grow as a result of this experience.

For even though mankind's society be revised from one end to the other, all who listen to God's will shall grow and profit thereby, regardless of the nature of their individual role in the process of mass action. They will follow God's will, and society *will change.*

It has been decided, long ago.

# ESSAY 64

*Received July 29, 1984*

Commonplace among people of His theological order is the notion of sin and evil, for it is through the involvement of a pretended alter ego of God known as Satan that some of the most important and substantive lessons of mankind are taught.

Satan, you see, is a myth, but a very useful myth specifically created by the North Country for the purpose of teaching basic perceptions of good and evil—right and wrong. For it is through the notion of Satan and evil that perceptions and training programs may be constructed wherein good may be contrasted against something that is non-good, or "evil." Good, you see, is an ephemeral quality that requires the contrast of something non-good in order to define and characterize the desirable attributes and perceptions which are inherent in the definition of good.

Good then defines a set of human values and characteristics which produce desirable or positive traits of the consciousness. Good then defines desired consciousness perceptions; evil defines the opposite. And Satan, as the allegorical spokesman of non-good or evil, assumes the role of a teaching implement wherein the attributes associated with non-good are associated with a cause—Satan himself.

Of course, Satan does not exist, nor has he ever. Nor has there ever been a "fallen angel," or any other such inhabitant of God's realm. Satan is a construct, an invention, designed to provide intermediate-level consciousness with an identifiable cause for the source of that which they were required to perceive as non-good. The cause was designed to appear hateful, disgusting, and vehemently distasteful, plus all associated myths were allowed to flourish. The reason? To decry, defile, hate, and despise the very thought of any perception *not on the good or desired perception list.*

Satan is therefore allegorical for that which is not desirable as a consciousness trait. And to fully define that which is not desirable, one must create it in abundance and fully expose each and every developing consciousness to each and every undesirable facet, for such exposure creates positive perceptions concerning positive or desired attributes. Good is ephemeral; it must be contrasted with evil in order to define good to the developing consciousness.

Hell is an equally purposeful construct, allegorically referring to the imagined undesirable final state of those who do not strive to pattern themselves about good. It is, of course, only a construct, and does not exist at any level of reality. There are, as described earlier, some consciousnesses who do not develop properly and are left to self-extinguish, but the incidence of this is extremely low. No, most consciousness evolves properly—some slower, some faster, but most evolve at some positive rate. And evil helps to shape their perceptions of right and wrong. It differentiates between appropriate and inappropriate behavior. It *teaches,* much as a teacher utilizes punishment or disapproval to differentiate proper behavior from improper behavior in a child.

Evil, Satan, and all the related allegory and imagery are pageant; they are all intentional constructs developed by the North Country and decreed by God. Evil, or non-good, is an essential element of the rich teaching fabric currently operating on earth. Evil is planned, administered, and activated by the North Country in the same manner as all other portions of the lesson plan for mankind.

Evil helps you learn to become good.

# ESSAY 65

*Received July 29, 1984*

After eons of waiting for the initial output of His earth system, God found all He had expected to be materializing and more. For as He had anticipated the development of technology, He had also anticipated the fertile fields it would create. By its very nature, technology works hand in hand with commerce to envelop a highly dynamic, interactive, and growing social fabric.

"Moab"[1]—or science and technology—began to produce a discernable effect very early in the development process, with North Country input providing the initial technological stimuli to invention and discovery. "Tyre"[1] developed appropriately later, providing the organization of government to society. "Sidon,"[1] a branch or subset of Tyre, evolved as bureaucracy was introduced to government as a purported aid to efficiency that efficiently added to the stress of the system.

"Edom"[1] followed shortly, with its complex fabric of

---

[1]*Moab, Tyre, Sidon, Edom:* Biblical allegory terms for the stress crucibles described.

interrelated stresses of medical technology and the disease and suffering it attempts to alleviate.

Constantly evolving stress was, of course, the desired nature of the plan, and it functioned magnificently. Stress crucible built upon stress crucible, until commerce, finance, medicine, government, religion—all were properly established and functioning well. And then came theological stress-test crucibles of advanced and sophisticated natures, and things began to accelerate and improve rapidly. The system for new man was not only functioning well, it was exceeding all expectations, and our delight was unbounded.

The Catholic Church—"Assyria"[2]—was the largest and most effective stress-test crucible implanted in modern times. With it one could guide entry-level consciousness into experiences and perceptions of God that were entirely erroneous but nevertheless effective and appropriate for their level of learning. And as the awareness of the consciousness developed after multiple life spans, the incorrigibly, obviously improper distortions of the Catholic Church would help to create desirable realizations in the more advanced consciousness, providing yet another valuable teaching service at that level.

At the entry level, therefore, Assyria would help orient the consciousness new to mankind, and assist the development of appropriate entry-level perceptions using the inelegant, nonsubtle approach of fear and doctrine—the perfect approach, of course, for an entry-level individual.

Later in one's development process, the very same Church could become the vehicle by which one's percep-

---

[2]*Assyria:* Biblical allegory term for the Catholic Church. See also *The First Book of the Lamb,* Chapters 12-17.

tions were matured to an internal awareness of the fundamental wrongness of the Church and its precepts, for it would become apparent to the target consciousness that there was something—somewhere—*wrong* about the Church's teachings and requirements. Finally, one's consciousness would mature to the level of sufficient perceptions concerning the Catholic Church that one would leave the Church—intellectually, if not physically—and become theologically *independent*.

But waiting beyond that level are the even more sophisticated theological cookers of modern times. All organized religions, all organized faiths, all organized religious doctrine from Judaism and Buddhism to Reverend Moon and Mormonism are intentionally distorted, partial revelations of the truth, with each intended to produce important effects within its targeted range of consciousness development.

Each and every theological movement on earth is a North Country production. Each is determined as a significant component of the total fabric of theological doctrine. Each is part of the whole.

It takes them all, to organize human consciousness into its final form. And they have all done their job well.

# ESSAY 66

*Received July 31, 1984*

Culminating a period of intense discomfort, theological evolution finally reached a plateau of knowing within a century or two of the Jesus incarnation, for it was at that very time that the third graduating class was moved into high gear, as it were, and placed on a painful but profitable path to its ultimate glory.

The churches that were to develop from the seeds planted in the time of Jesus would have profound effects upon their advanced pupils as they and the theological doctrines developed simultaneously, side by side. It was, however, an effort of incredible complexity to simultaneously create the stress doctrines and maneuver and guide the stressees accordingly as they progressed from life to life and theological experience to theological experience.

Martin Luther represented a large deviation of the theological structure, creating, as it were, a rift of monumental proportions in the churches of the day. Incredibly determined, Martin Luther was a typical example of North Country infiltration of the system by an advanced, mature consciousness in order to effect some change of significant proportions. In such a case it is vital that a mature consciousness perform the task, since functional perceptive communication is all-important to correctly guiding the task to its proper conclusion.

Martin Luther was but one example of many mature consciousnesses incarnating to perform specific tasks regarding the direction of mankind. Many have performed this duty over the centuries, efficiently providing mature communicative paths to the development of significant social, political, or theological change.

Presidents, kings, politicians, ministers—many who have participated in significant change have been intentional infiltrations of a mature consciousness possessing mature communicative perceptions, and it has been through the efforts of such as these that society has been inexorably guided on its path from crisis to crisis, major change to major change.

Theology is guided by several forces, with doctrine being only one. Even more important is the base information, or written word of God upon which the theologies are based. As it is known by now, such input to the system is provided through incarnate, advanced consciousnesses who are especially trained to provide this function. All theological base lines are drawn in this way, with deviations therefrom caused through the activity and efforts of mature consciousnesses who are guided by the North Country in their roles.

The Sons of God represent the most advanced consciousness level which presently incarnates on earth. Ancient consciousnesses created before the earth system formed, these advanced conscious intelligences are charged with the administration of God's system of consciousness production. It is these who incarnate in ultra-critical roles involving large modifications in the structure of earth's cultures, society, and doctrine. It is these who write the words of God that are required as theological base lines. And it is these who love mankind exceedingly, for they realize even when incarnate that something very special is within each human being—something very precious to their Creator.

It is these to whom the keys of the kingdom are truly given, for they are the first inheritors of God's glory. But theirs is not the only glory; each and every consciousness that matures will eventually partake of the same glory, and even more.

*All* grow toward a glory unbounded.

# ESSAY 67

*Received August 2, 1984*

There are hundreds of organized religious factions in the world today, all organized and operating under the guidance of the North Country. And there are several more which exist at our behest and operate not without guidance but with minimum guidance, for they are the religions of tomorrow, and they are only beginning. They are currently considered not even as religions, but as science, metaphysics, occult—and even politics.

For these fledgling groups are to draw succor, nourishment, and knowledge of His creation from the material now being transmitted to earth. They will be the counterpoints of tomorrow, each offering a different perspective on the fundamental truths now being provided. All will talk of Christ; all will speak of Heaven as a known realm of known characteristics; all will know, beyond any doubt, of the reality of each Christ's coming. And they will even know *how* he comes: in spirit, within his Lamb.

For with this generation are the heavens opened wide

for earth to see. The stars will "fall,"[1] for they are not real but images. Love will blossom as a new positive gateway to a paradise of knowledge, caring, and being. Mankind will itself graduate, in a way, for the knowledge and understanding of mankind will undertake quantum leaps of meaning.

The entire earth will know, and accept, the reality of my coming in flesh; but the world will learn of it after it has already happened. They will learn of the reality of the natural realm, of the nature of love and the love force, and of the constantly occurring creation of reality by loving, caring beings who are simply older and more advanced than you of earth. They will learn of the fundamental caring of their Creator, and furthermore learn of their own impending glory. Their rewards will be known in advance of their attainment, and the pressure to attain will rise astronomically. Good will absolutely triumph over evil as humanity learns the source of all intrusive emotion, thought, and deed. Love will surface as the single unifying theme of all brotherhoods of man, and the understanding and personal attainment of graduation day as the single most important constituent of life.

All will develop faster and more accurately as the now-higher average maturity of mankind enters a phase of outstanding love, caring, filial devotion, and God-oriented growth.

The fourth class is already forming, and its lesson plans have been laid. It waits only for word of its savior, and the knowledge of his coming, to blossom into the most won-

[1]Compare Matthew 24:29, also Revelation 6:13.

drous and incredible growth period ever experienced by the consciousness of man.

God is waiting, and His face has turned to you. The fourth generation will skyrocket toward glory, for it has been already decreed. It will happen, you may rest assured. And I will be there still—advising, helping, controlling, administering your rise to glory. I and the new team now forming. I and your Lamb, who even now prepares to assume my present role. We will, together, watch over you, nurture you, care for you; and when your time has come, he will come for you, even as I am doing now for those who precede you.

I am the Holy Ghost, your loving caretaker and administrator of God's plan on earth. I am love. And you are coming, soon—home to us.

# ESSAY 68

*Received August 3, 1984*


Fundamentally reduced to essentials, the future of mankind rests securely within the individual conscious psyche, or consciousness, of each person. For it is here, in the conscious, aware, inner self—the *consciousness*—that growth occurs, and it is here that the emphasis of the entire structure of reality exists.

Mankind is entering a phase of physical attainment and glory not previously experienced at any phase of earth's history, for this will be the first time since He initiated His system of consciousness production that sufficient consciousnesses have been matured to sufficient levels of awareness to physically implement that new society which is about to unfold.

Certainly, many fine minds will be deleted from the physical organization of mankind as a result of the current graduation of class number three, but there will be no net negative effect of this, for they will become a portion of the guiding light for generation number four; they *join* the ranks of those predecessors who guide and teach mankind from the natural realm. It is therefore expected that the natural increase of staff will enable us to provide a level of interactive guidance and growth-nurturing never before achievable since His system began.

No longer will limitations be imposed because of insufficient angel-power to "cover all the bases," for it is with the fourth generation that the system begins to develop self-sustaining characteristics. All future generations are therefore expected to provide a sufficient influx of mature consciousness to the natural realm such that self-sustainment is assured; i.e., there will no longer be a shortage of teachers for the size of the classes enrolled.

It is at this point, i.e., the time of the fourth generation (Abraham Covenant),[1] that the Sons of God will be released from future incarnation roles, for the ranks of mature consciousnesses will have grown and evolved to the level of providing mature guidance and control from the ranks of the system itself. Furthermore, it is expected that the life development experiences of the newly advanced consciousnesses who assume the critical managerial roles will enable them to better perform a most noble undertaking. They will, you see, have had personally developed through the very system they will be administrating.

Concurrently with the system developing a self-sustaining nature at the graduation of the fourth generation will be the consideration of possible scenarios by which the expansion of the total base (quantity) of consciousnesses is to be provided with grounds (planets) and school buildings (social structures) thereon. For it will then become the consuming obligation of the Sons of God to provide for the natural expansion of His incredibly successful plan, as the develop-

---

[1]The Covenant with Abraham will be found in Genesis 15:13-16.

ment of mature consciousness begins to take on massive proportions.

It is not presently known what the final outcome or answer will be, for administration of the current system saps our available creative resources, requiring all we have to give and a little more in addition. After the fourth generation rises to their glory, we will begin serious consideration of the alternatives involved. Planetary expansion, new races, increasing of performance requirements in existing species and races, totally new species, possible scenarios involving God-oriented natural laws to become usable on earth through modification of earth's current reality—all are possibilities, and all will be considered.

As caretakers of His system our task continually magnifies, and His glory continually magnifies with its unbounded growth and success.

# ESSAY 69

*Received August 3, 1984*

Although it has been determined from of old, the Sons of God are nevertheless excited about the approaching scenario. It is, you see, the first major successes in the system that are now occurring, for it is with generation number three that the output has become large, and it is with generation number four that the system will become self-sustaining.

Pleasure, for those of us administering His system, is the knowledge of a task well done, and the blossoming of His system attests to its success. We are pleased, and He is pleased. And earth shall be pleased, as it becomes commonplace knowledge that earth and mankind and all life are melting pots, formative crucibles, and the very origin of the creation of advanced godlike conscious intelligences—individuals whose aspirations may exceed all imagination.

It is for these—the consciousnesses of earth who developed through His system—that special delights await as they discover, one by one, the incredible truth of His creation and His unbounded joy in their existence.

Wonder will follow wonder as mankind blossoms and

reaches toward a God and godhood itself that are finally real and attainable.

Earth will no longer be simply a nursery; it will become a full-fledged school with complete and glorious understanding of what lies beyond the schoolyard gate. And the achievable glory of mankind will be unbounded.

# ESSAY 70

*Received August 4, 1984*

Now we shall address the most significant topic of the current theological world: the book of the Revelation to John. For it is within this revelation that the last days of this cycle are described in rather surprising terms; surprising, at least, to the staid theologians of planet earth.

For the Revelation to John (which I recorded, by the way, in my John the Baptist incarnation) deals not with fiery serpents, dragons, and massive physical catastrophes. No, it deals primarily with physical response to emotional and mental anguish of unprecedented levels. It tells of a time—the very time coming upon you now—when the theological belief system will be totally demolished by understanding of the true nature of the reality in which you exist. It speaks of man at war with himself as he struggles to perceive the truth in a bitter sea of conflicting testimony, information, opinion, and half-truths. It refers to the anguish of separation from the status quo of earth's believed physical reality. It describes the laity as they espouse new things previously unheard of, and the clergy as they follow suit. It describes Catholics, Jews, Christians,

Buddhists—any and all people of earth as they wrestle with profound change in their system of belief and their very understanding of reality. And in the end, they will each and every one come to the point of recognizing the validity of their inner guidance for the thing that it really is: *communication.* Loving, caring, guiding, nurturing *direction* directly from the North Country to the living intellect of each and every man, woman, and child on earth.[1]

Next to the nature of the shocks imposed, the actual remaining underlying meanings of the Revelation to John are almost trivial, for they refer allegorically to the things we have already discussed either here or in *The First Book of the Lamb.* The seven letters to the seven churches,[2] for instance, are specifically organized to address the incarnate Sons of God who are in need of unconfounding, for the messages are specifically oriented for them to relate to in a manner consistent with their confounded personalities. The seven churches are the Sons of God on earth, and the current Lamb—my firstborn—is among them. To him is addressed certain of the statements regarding "he who conquers"[3] within these letters, for to him goes the mantle of Holy Ghost for the next generation—number four—the one now commencing. He is your next lord and savior; he will be he who comes for class number four, even as I am

---

[1]Compare Jeremiah 31:31-33, New King James Version: "Behold, the days are coming, says the LORD, when I will make a new covenant ... I will put my law in their minds ...."

[2]Revelation 2, 3.

[3]Within the biblical allegory, the verb *to conquer* (also translated *to overcome*) refers to the overcoming of physical reality; it therefore applies, depending upon context and tense, to current graduates, past graduates, or Sons of God. It is also used in the sense of one who *leads* those who conquer, i.e., *a conqueror.* The "he who conquers" ("he who overcomes" in King James) statements in these letters refer variously to this entire range of individuals.

coming for class number three. He will be your teacher and your administrator, and I will be his teacher, even as my predecessor has been my teacher and his predecessor his teacher.

Often misunderstood by theologians, Christ is not, you see, a physical being. The statements in *The First Book of the Lamb* relating to my impending incarnation as Christ were intentionally misleading; not to create an error in fact, but more accurately to inform you of the bizarre (for you at this stage) truth of your reality in measured, acceptable doses. Had you been given the full truth in one single step, the shock would have been great. This, then, is an example of successively enlarging frames of reference yielding successively more-true truths, as previously described. *Christ* is actually a euphemism—a carrot dangled on the end of a stick—a grand promise expressed in easy-to-comprehend physical terms.

But the reality of Christ is even more outstandingly wonderful, for Christ does not come to you physically; you go to him, when you graduate. And it is in the natural realm that his government is established and where you serve him, as you join the team that administrates, nurtures, loves, and develops the still-immature consciousnesses of earth.

# ESSAY 71

*Received August 6, 1984*


Frequently considered to be savior of mankind, Jesus Christ was not portrayed within the Bible in a necessarily true literal manner. For although he indeed was the promised savior, the mechanism of the system was not revealed, leaving those who followed to believe Jesus Christ was the savior of the current generation.

This is, of course, not the fact. Allegorically, Jesus saved the world. Actually, he was my Father and I his firstborn, and as the then-current Holy Ghost he appeared to the physical world through me, during my incarnation as John (the Baptist). Jesus did not come physically for his redeemed. He appeared within my incarnate body in the same manner as I now appear within my Lamb's body. He wrote through me even as I now write through my first-born, who has incarnated for this purpose even as I did, two thousand years ago.

Jesus exists, of course; he is my Father, as I am Father to your Lamb, my firstborn. And as I write these words through his hand, Jesus—my Father—supervises and

watches over the expanding wonder of the graduation of
the third generation. He is with you; I am with you; your
Lamb is with you; and all will be with you in Heaven.

*The Lamb,* you see, is an honorary title, much like *Christ.*
Whereas Christ signifies one who is currently in charge of
the administration of mankind, the Lamb is the one who
follows in his stead. I am Christ—Holy Ghost—of the third
generation. Your Lamb succeeds me during the period of
the fourth generation, and then his Lamb will succeed him.

And so it continues, with Lamb—Holy Ghost—Christ—
God—all consciousness continually evolving, no matter
what level is considered. Roach consciousnesses evolve to
flying things; dog consciousnesses evolve to tigers; human
consciousnesses evolve to maturity in Heaven; past graduates evolve; Christ evolves; God evolves.

Christ means savior; Christ means reigning Holy Ghost;
Christ means the particular Son of God who administrates
and manages the earth system for an entire generation, or
the period of a graduating class. Christ is savior for he
brings, at the close of the age, knowledge and awareness
of their impending glory to the graduates of the system.

He also brings something quite different for those who
are to remain on earth: for those consciousnesses who are
not yet mature, he brings the promise of yet another
graduation day—*their* graduation. He introduces them to
the heavenly administration team for the succeeding generation; he provides the written words the new generation
will need in their rise to glory; and he establishes the new
path decreed for the society of man. Two thousand years
is a long time for a given social structure; change is decreed,
for the fourth generation possesses attributes in abundance
as never before on earth. The system is *working,* and social

183

restructuring is necessary to provide a new optimum environment for the maturing consciousness of man.

The fourth generation is convening, and society will be required to provide the environment it needs. It has been decreed by God.

# ESSAY 72

*Received August 7, 1984*

Love is the one element of God's creation that, above all else, is sacrosanct—*holy*—to the inhabitants of His natural realm. For it is with love that one creates, breathes, offers succor, and gives rest. It is love that composes the very stuff of matter, for in its love-force implementation it becomes the heart and soul of the matter creation technique developed by God. It is through the love of the Creator that we in His natural realm partake of His blessings and participate in His glory. It is through His love that all matter and all three-dimensional apparent energies are maintained. It is through His love that the very world continues to exist from one moment to the next, with the creation of each moment's reality being a complete and separate effort from the prior moment's reality.

The love of the Creator is not automatic; it, and the creation or maintenance of matter in your reality, is freely given by Him for us to manipulate to your benefit, that you may grow to godhood and someday be all that He has learned to become. And when that day comes, He will have learned even more for you to know; leading, teaching, loving, as He blazes the trail before you to godhood and the wonders of a limitless, glorious eternity. God is love, you see, in a very real sense, for He is the source of love. All love, all creative energy in the natural realm, flows from Him and returns to Him. He is our dynamo, our propulsion, our teacher.

And He is already learning new things for us to know—new wonders—as He, too, continues to evolve; and continues to love, even more than before.

# ESSAY 73

*Received August 7, 1984*

All life in His natural realm comes from Him, for all have been created by Him. In His own way and in His own time has each and every one of us been brought to conscious awareness, then conscious maturity, through His processes of growth and creation. Each Son of God was originally created as a special preproduction or prototype consciousness; "handmade," if you will, using fundamental creative processes to grow, develop, and bring into full conscious awareness the first of God's intelligent creations.

As He continued to develop and refine, the Sons of God grew, developed, and refined, until eventually they had evolved to levels wherein the creative process was also within their scope of ability. By then God Himself had evolved further and had borne the concept of the earth-matter-reality system of consciousness breeding. He laid forth the plan and described it, but its implementation was left to us. The Sons of God, using their knowledge of creation as supplied and taught by God, *implemented* His plan, causing matter to form, earth to form, rivers to flow, and bodies to grow. Flowers, trees, insects, humans, animals—all were brought into being by His initially formed consciousnesses, who are known as the Sons of God (*Elohim*).[1]

It is they who have developed the lesson plans, who have implemented them since the earth was formed, and who have incarnated, time and time again, to implement critical portions of the development plan for man. Incarnating in roles requiring perceptions of superhuman levels and inherent, fully developed communicative (with the North Country) skills, the Sons of God who incarnate submit themselves to the same rules imposed by the system as those whom they serve: their memories are scrubbed clean while they are incarnate. Furthermore, they are lovingly but continuously provided a constant flow of thoughts, perceptions, feelings, and emotions that serve to confuse and confound them during their incarnation. They are totally under outside control, so that their missions within physical reality may be guided and implemented with the full capabilities of the North Country. When a Son of God incarnates to perform a necessary task in physical reality, he becomes a tool, an implement, of the Holy Ghost. An extension that can thereby affect the flow of physical reality by apparently normal means—by causes and persons *apparently* within the system.

---

[1]*Elohim:* Ancient Hebrew word for "Gods."

# ESSAY 74

*Received August 13, 1984*

Perhaps the most significant method of teaching consciousness to become more involves the duplication of perceptions created during confrontive renditions of reality.

Reality, you see, involves more than merely being in a state of existence; it also includes the very essence of one's creaturehood. It is in this environment composed of living creatures that many of the most significant lessons occur, for it is when one confronts a reality that appears inescapable that the most valid lessons are learned. Confrontations cause a "hard" reality from which there are no apparent avenues of escape less than the path ahead.

Less than actual reality, perhaps, real situations are nevertheless caused to appear to be consistent with the imagined or understood circumstances surrounding the event. Furthermore, events are focused to bring the desired confrontation into eminent position, such that its avoidance becomes impossible.

Confrontations are therefore a prime educational tool in the vast storehouse of possible teaching mechanisms incorporated into mankind's social fabric. With confrontation one may incur the teaching of serious value perceptions which are not possible otherwise. Confrontations with death, evil, useless platitude, organized counter-effort, sickness, distress—all are mechanisms in which the target consciousness is intentionally and willfully placed into a confrontive circumstance from which he cannot escape without first enduring the confrontation. His entire being will become fully absorbed in the confrontation, as massive personal growth—*consciousness* growth—is achieved during the experience of confrontation, pain, enduring, understanding, and finally *overcoming* in whatever sense is appropriate for the lesson plan involved.

Confrontations are therefore lesson culminating points, wherein the final organization of a host of preparatory perceptions are brought into final concrete form as a single advanced perception cell. This then can be duplicated, in a similar situation, by a process involving modification of the original perception to yet another of similar properties which however acts in a different perceptive framework or mechanism.

In such a way can needed advanced perception cells be synthesized from one which is similar yet not identical and which exists in a different perceptive framework or organization. First the confrontive experience creates the basal advanced perception, then similar-yet-different circumstances are developed to maneuver the original perception into the form of other needed, functionally similar, advanced perception cells.

Cells of vast complexity may be thus created, using a single confrontive experience to synthesize the original complex perception from which duplicate perceptive cells are created and subsequently modified by exposure to relatively similar events and processes.

Perception cells do not grow unaided; their existence occurs as the result of extremely careful implementation of personal and mass lesson plans. These cells are synthesized at great effort during confrontive episodes of great stress, uncertainty, or other overpowering mental or emotional circumstance.

Mental turmoil, illness, and disarray are not random illnesses of a physical being. They are *lessons*—complex, sophisticated, and needed for the consciousness to grow.

# ESSAY 75

*Received August 14, 1984*

We may now embark upon an experience of mind, for it is now the time to consider elements of one's conscious self.

For it is within the conscious mind—the conscious intellect—the *consciousness*—that all thought, memory, knowing, and being occurs. It is within the consciousness that *existence* occurs, for consciousness is being alive as a self-sustaining, existent, individual element of creation.

It is more than mere existence, however. Consciousness is loving control of your environment. It is loving, nurturing, and changing the things about you. It is knowing. It is God. It is each one of us. And it is you.

All living things contain a consciousness at some level of developmental maturity. All living things provide connection of the consciousness to physical reality for the unique purpose of developing, training, and forming the consciousness contained. And it is with this sole purpose—development, growth, and forming of mature consciousness—that the earth and mankind have been formed.

# ESSAY 76

*Received August 15, 1984*

Now we shall explore more of the mysteries of the mind, in which and by which all matter and energy exist.

For it is with the mind—the conscious intellect—that all things exist, whether matter, three-dimensional, multidimensional, or other organization of complex states of being. *Mind,* in the context used here, means the operative mechanism of the mature conscious intelligence—the *intellect* of a conscious intelligence or consciousness.

"Mind over matter" is indeed a perception of grand proportions, for it is the mature mind which organizes and constructs living, sentient God-forces into the organized masses or constructs known to you as matter and reality.

Mind denotes control to a level unknown by mankind, for it denotes not only the creative ability but the ability to *be.* Many various forms of being-perspective are associated with advanced states of conscious development, such that advanced organizations of dimension can be brought within the physical (in a manner of speaking) boundaries of one's conscious self. Godhood is achieved, of course, through such advanced states of development, maturing, and being-perception.

Although within the reach of all, godhood may not necessarily be actually achieved by all, since a constant self-imposed regimen of striving to perceive is needed to develop one's perceptions on the continuing basis required.

Struggling to perceive is therefore a basic tenet of our lesson processes on earth, for it is of utmost importance that the developing consciousness be taught the need for *constantly* struggling to perceive. It is through incorporation of this tenet as a basic personality characteristic that the promise of godhood becomes achievable to the conscious intellect. Perceptions are the key element in one's own developmental program, for one must constantly and continuously struggle to perceive—to *know*, deep inside, the fundamental-appearing truths that are just beyond his grasp. And if you do try, if you do attempt to constantly perceive that which is just beyond your seeming perceptions, you will grow—and *fast*, for you will have become consciously fixed upon the one thing most important to your personal development and your own promise of godhood.

*Struggle to perceive,* and you will.

# ESSAY 77

*Received August 16, 1984*

Love is perceived by the world as a wholly ephemeral aspect of human existence. Considered as some element of reproductive necessity on one hand, and as an element of brotherhood, grace, and filial devotion on the other, love is widely misunderstood by humanity.

Love is, as I have oft repeated, the very stuff of conscious existence. It is life, breath, grace, caring, nurturing—even *creating*. It is our communication, our tenderness, the basis of our desire for perfection as loving beings. Love is enhancing the quality of existence. Love is giving to others that which nurtures them. Love is knowing that love is real and that it is uniquely valuable to the mature conscious intellect. Without love, we would cease to be; we would wither away.

Love's ultimate value to mankind is in its value to the emerging consciousness of man. Without it one withers and dies; with it one achieves the very pinnacles of glory.

Love is therefore the most important of all the perceptions to be developed within the budding consciousness. It

195

prepares one for existence; it mediates one's eternal soul; it prepares one for *life*.

God has purposed for each of us a glorious immortal existence in which all the lessons learned on earth come into full confluence as a complete, unique, and loving personality. As on earth, each and every consciousness is an individual—a separate, completely unique and independent being of great conscious awareness. And as life's lessons learned as man, as woman, as child, as elder merge and blend into one glorious, composite, perfect whole, thereby has your consciousness learned, accreted, stored, and become all that it is: a unique, loving inhabitant of God's natural realm. A mature consciousness, *resplendent* with the grace and love purposed by his Creator.

# ESSAY 78

*Received August 19, 1984*

Necessary on the surface, the lion's share of earth's governmental structures relentlessly require more than their share of taxpayer support.

Between these structures and the people they serve lie the institutions by which mankind truly prospers: the theologically structured organizations of earth. For it is through the churches that mankind has grown and prospered, not through the governments. The churches of earth have relentlessly produced and provided the specific level of non sequitur, confusion, hopefulness, and—*something else*—that drives the flocks they represent forward through fear, doctrine, malcontentment, zeal—whatever motivating factor is appropriate for the consciousnesses served.

For it is the churches that stand up for God, even when there is pitifully little evidence of His existence for humans to see. It is the churches that demonstrate the probable existence of things too wonderful to hope for. It is the churches and the men and women who serve them who relentlessly exemplify the caring, nurturing individual who

197

performs the duties that feel *right* deep down inside, no matter what aspects of conventional wisdom he or she may violate. Doing what is right—perceiving it and doing it, no matter what others may say—this is the essence of the example set by persons of the cloth.

They are personally beset, of course, by numerous doubts and intentionally inflicted (by us) lacks of what they perceive as being necessary information and understanding; yet they persevere in their unusually nonconforming roles, risking their entire apparent physical well-being to satisfy some ephemeral inner knowing that what they do is *right,* no matter what.

It is, of course, this very perception of "right, deep down inside" that exemplifies the true leader of men, for it is only well-advanced consciousnesses who have developed this inner perception to such a high degree that they are virtually incapable of ignoring their internal perceptions. Due to a lack of information, of course, they each tend to identify the process within themselves in a different way, but all sense the same thing: a deep internal knowing of what they must do.

And it is this example of one performing unusually nonconforming functions within society, while feeling deeply that he *must* do them, that creates the finest example of God-oriented mature behavior for the people. Preachers know not why they do what they do; they offer reasons, excuses, personal tales of being called by visions, dreams, inner voices—none, of course, understand why they feel so right about what they do. They do not know that they are an example for earth; that they exemplify the following of one's inner voices—one's conscience—for all to see.

Preachers, ministers, priests do not understand their roles on earth. They do not realize why or what they are. They do not understand that they are examples of doing what feels right, deep down inside—*regardless.*

# ESSAY 79

*Received August 19, 1984*

Normally considered essential to spiritual growth, prayer offers little of perceived value to the aspiring Christian, Moslem, or Jew. Prayer, you see, does not do what it is vaguely purported to do within the scriptures. Prayer is not necessary to speak with God or with any inhabitant of the natural realm. Prayer is obviously a construct for the purpose of creating a privately considered state of mind during which one's awareness of outside intervention might be heightened. Prayer serves no useful purpose in the conventional sense, since God and I can "tune in" to individual thought and perception processes regardless of the intent of the individual. It is through constant monitoring of an individual consciousness that his growth process is administered; prayer adds nothing to the knowledge of the person already available.

Prayer does accomplish one highly significant function, though, and it is for this reason and this reason alone that it has been introduced within the system: Prayer teaches communicative awareness. It stimulates and enhances the perception that something—somehow—some*one* may be really there, and may even be *listening.* Completely one-sided, then, is the practice of prayer; it represents no level of communication greater than normally attained with the developing consciousness. It does, however, teach the reality—or *possibility*—of something more, if one could only perceive it!

Prayer stretches one's perceptions of reality. Prayer connects one's perceptions of God to his reality. Prayer strengthens and supports one's inherent knowledge of right and wrong, for it lends credence to the inner knowing of something—somewhere—if it could only be perceived!

Prayer is important; it makes one *grow.*

# ESSAY 80

*Received August 19, 1984*


Needless to say, the state of knowledge within the world is suddenly enriching by this massive influx of information concerning the natural reality in which we all live, for it is here and now that history will record as the beginning of an enlightened age of man, with knowledge replacing supposition and myth.

For it is with the culmination of the third generation, and the beginning of the fourth, that mankind enters upon a stage of development unlike anything even philosophized upon the earth. Space, time, reality—all constructs of your world will become known for what they really are: loving, nurturing, intentional constructs of a loving, nurturing, *advanced* state of existence.

Knowledge will take on entirely new forms as the reality of a multidimensional cosmos replete with advanced beings becomes integrated into mankind's fabric of understanding. Knowledge of the Creator (God); knowledge of His unbounded, loving, caring, nurturing intellect; knowledge of godhood; knowledge of sin and evil for the teaching mechanisms they are; knowledge of the *real* reality will literally cause man to explode with understanding as the age of yet another new man dawns.

Unlike anything you have ever dreamed or even suspected during flights of imagination, the future of physical mankind is bright—*resplendent* with the care and nurturing of a superior realm whose children are the living creatures of earth. Mankind will grow in ways never anticipated and at rates never imagined.

Another new age has dawned, and with it, another step for man.

# ESSAY 81

*Received August 19, 1984*

Common among mankind are notions or perceptions of time and space. Also known are dimensions, although perceptions have not been previously permitted to extend significantly beyond the barest minimum.

One of the tremendous increases in the knowledge of new man will relate to the reality of multiple—*infinite*—dimensions of awareness and being. Although significant primarily to the inhabitant of the natural realm, the knowledge of multiple dimensions will yield important effects for the understanding of your physical system. Knowledge will heap upon knowledge as simple realizations blossom into full-fledged scientific awarenesses. Entire scientific establishments and cultures will modify extensively, almost overnight, as realizations settle into proper perspective. God will assume new meaning as man discovers a benevolent, fair, and loving Creator who will provide all that is *appropriate* to the developing consciousnesses of earth.

Birds, beasts, and man will become recognized for what they are: varying segments of the spectrum of creation of consciousness. The beast will truly lie down with the lion as the entire earth becomes intuitively aware of the inherent equality of consciousness. Children are cared for because they are young and inexperienced; likewise must the beast be cared for, for he is only just learning that which you have already mastered. He and you are the same; only time is the difference, only experience, only growth. For even as God is superior to the consciousnesses of man and yet cares for them, so must man care for those less evolved than he. Fairness, equanimity, moderation, but coupled with understanding of the beast's role in the development of mature consciousness. He, too, will inherit the kingdom of God one day. He, too, will bear children and endure the hardships of mankind one day. He, too, is a brother under the skin.

He is just less mature than you. And you can help your brother grow.

# ESSAY 82

*Received August 19, 1984*

Perhaps another facet of human awareness development that is to become prominent relates to the practice and acceptance of political process, for it is through political process that nations, peoples, and governments seemingly ebb and flow in a ceaseless, undulating sea of relentless change and modification.

Political process, as I am certain you can perceive by now, represents an enormously useful and positive means by which the North Country is able to construct constantly changing realities for mankind. A process replete with perceptions of constituents, leaders, and peoples, it is the very fabric of the social structure it supports. It is also a direct means of modifying that structure, therefore it is in relatively constant use by the North Country for the implementation of revised social characteristics.

Political processes, especially within the Western nations, provide a virtual thoroughfare to the transmission and development of social change, for complex social structures are easily altered through adjustment of the perceptions of both leaders and constituents.

Politics, therefore, is one of the least of all human endeavors in which free will is allowed to be exercised free of interference. Although free will is tantamount to a law of nature within His system, society-related structures are effectively manipulated into being through modification of perception. Free will is always allowed to flourish unabated, but in the event of a desired social change through political process, the *perceptions* of the leaders and constituents are affected—they are given those perceptions which will cause their exercise of free will to produce the desired results.

Society is thus dramatically controlled by process of perception modification. Allowing constant exercise of free will, such situations are controlled through modification of apparent reality—what one *thinks* he hears, sees, or understands. And it shall always be thus, regardless of the development of mankind. Regardless of the growth of knowledge and wisdom, we shall always maneuver your society into the desired framework or structure. Political process is, always has been, and always will be a North Country production. We know what you need, to incur optimum growth of your conscious selves.

And that is exactly what you shall have.

# ESSAY 83

*Received August 20, 1984*

Political means are frequently used to establish, on earth, the directions of social structures such as kingdoms, empires, etc. What I mean is that politics play an important role in establishing the desired social order, for it is through modification of political process by means of adjusting perceptions that great social structures are both formed and disentrailed.

Political process provides an apparent real structure to the development of a particular social order. It generates needed artifacts of reality so that the social structure thus obtained appears to be based upon sound physical facts and figures, i.e., physical historical fact that one can point to in physical reality.

Much like most aspects of your reality, however, the truth of the matter is, like Edom, that we have set about to cause not only the needed social order but to simultaneously provide a physically identifiable cause for the existence of that order. Part of the trauma associated with politics is the real lack of anything definite for the politician to gauge his campaign oratory upon. In a free society, the politician must *perceive* what is necessary to say, for the combined analyses of all possible predecessors leave one hopelessly without a solid analytical understanding of political process.

What is the missing element? The North Country. We affect the perceptions of the constituents who popularize a certain political cadre, and we also affect the perceptions of the politicians accordingly. There is no more a cause and effect relationship between political structures and the social structures they serve or represent than there is a cause and effect relationship between illness and medicine. We cause the apparent cause, and then we cause the effect. We cause them *both,* to create an apparent closed system of reality in which you learn, totally unaware of the larger reality that surrounds you.

Politics represents a major element of North Country endeavor, for it embraces entire major aspects of social awareness and structure. Politics and government portray an element of mankind's social fabric that is dynamic, forceful, and the ideal means of creating, maintaining, and adjusting the social interactions of man.

# ESSAY 84

*Received August 20, 1984*

Now we shall consider the subject of human conflict on massive scales: war, civil strife, and the necessity of mass conflict during the development of man.

For it is the instigators of such conflict—the individuals responsible—that are generally the least responsible, for they are portraying an image; they are developing the mass conflict scenario we require.

War is deplorable to the rational human, and for its full deplorable nature to be in evidence, one must experience war. Not since the beginnings of the current era has man been without war, for its formative nature creates positive perceptions of good and caring among those it affects.

The initial perceptions, of course, are of horror, disgust, and dismay. Following these are shock and sometimes surrender, but always follows a period of growth through the positive perceptions of the enhanced value of mutual trust, kindness, and love.

Like sin, evil, and illness, man must be provided with the negative aspects of war in order to fully and properly

210

frame his notions concerning good, or the desirable characteristics of consciousness. Thus does man grow, albeit
somewhat bloodied and bowed, but he—the inner essential
man that is temporarily wearing the bloodied and bowed
body—he *grows*. And the growth is substantial, for exposure to broad-scale conflict is a massive confrontive episode
that befalls each consciousness only once or twice in his
experience on earth.

It is a necessary confrontive experience, for it teaches
lessons that can be taught no other way. War enhances and
underscores the value of filial devotion, brotherly and
sisterly love, trust, and caring, for it is a supreme example
of the incredibly terrible nature of characteristics in opposi-
tion with these. Contempt for fellow man, conquest, the
need to succeed or gain personal power at the expense of
others, cruelty—all negative human aspects are brought
into such sharp focus by the conflict of war that the
consciousness learns the true value of the nobler characteristics of man. And by learning them he grows, for these
perceptions are not only espoused by his conscious mind,
they become part of his very conscious fabric—his consciousness itself.

War has represented a portion of human endeavor that
has been difficult for us to implement, for we know the
lessons are difficult ones. But in the knowledge of the
indestructible immortal consciousness and the continuity
of His loving development and growth of consciousness
lies the understanding of this reprehensible mechanism of
human endeavor. War must be understood as a means to
an end—understood as proper process in the development
of one's consciousness. It is such a massive confrontive
experience that it efficiently synthesizes needed perceptual

211

cells that might otherwise require several lifetimes of lesser experiences.

One must be exposed to evil in order to define that which is good and to furthermore instigate the positive awareness and growth of positive perceptions; good is desired feverishly after confrontation with evil. And war serves the same master—the individual, growing consciousness who must be exposed to all possible negative, nondesired traits of consciousness in a way that causes the growth and development of desired traits, characteristics, and perceptions. War is reprehensible, especially if you've experienced it. And if you have, you've grown from the experience.

But if you had not been exposed to it, you would not have grown. Life would not be so precious, love so important, caring and nurturing so valuable to you.

War has been difficult; but it has been necessary, for you to grow.

# ESSAY 85

*Received August 20, 1984*

Perhaps the most difficult aspect of mortal confrontation lies in the mind of man, for it is extremely uncomfortable for a well-developed consciousness to be a party to personal mortal confrontation.

Such things as bullying of lesser individuals, war, violence, mortal conflict—all heavily weigh on the conscience of a developed conscious intellect.

These responses are to be expected, for mortal conflict is used to further enhance the perceptions of its bestial or low natural level. Such conflicts incur a desire in one to rise above the level of such conflict at any cost or effort, thereby creating a great positive influx of emotions and attitudes supporting the desired final perceptions.

For such confrontations are caused, of course, to make you grow. They are part of the stress fabric upon which the present educational system is based. Stress puts you under pressure to perceive that which transcends the stressful situation, and when you do perceive the new transcending level, it becomes a part of you. The new, more advanced perception assumes its place in the organization of your consciousness and becomes a part of you, forever.

Stress and confrontation are very difficult to administer, let alone endure. We would rather it hadn't been necessary—the stress—but there was no other way. Now, with society more advanced, the older stresses will give way to new ones more specifically configured to optimize the growth of a more developed people. The increased average consciousness level of mankind will largely affect the stresses employed, and many changes will be made within society to implant more sophisticated stress mechanisms.

Mankind is advancing, and so are its lesson plans.

# ESSAY 86

*Received August 26, 1984*

Now we shall involve our discussions in the issue of abortion, for it is this issue that most oppresses the fair sex of the land at this time.

Abortion, you see, is a means to an end, as are all implements of the earth educational system. It is for the mothers to strive and struggle that abortion was conceived. Based in the elemental love of a mother for her child, abortion serves to stretch one's perceptions beyond the boundaries of the normally perceived reality.

Abortion is tailored to provide, as an issue, a growing public awareness of the reality of the soul or consciousness. Only through utilization of mass media in a controversial way can large numbers of individuals be embroiled in such a communicative manner. Only through issues such as these may public attention be focused tightly on important areas of perception, for it is the perception of consciousness—of soul—of *self*—for which the abortion issue is raised in society.

Abortion is a great issue within today's cultural elite—

those of Babylon[1]—for it strikes at the heart of their most consuming inner need, or area of sensed nonfulfillment: *What am I and how am I here?* Where do I go? *Why* am I here? Abortion as an issue raises these questions among the public outcry and causes them to develop the credibility associated with mass concern and interest. Abortion serves the need of focusing the masses upon the potential (to them) reality of the consciousness. It fits hand in hand with the structuring of consciousness-awareness perceptions being developed through the media and among political campaigns currently in progress. UFO's; Reagan's religious views; abortion; motion pictures concerning strange apparitions and hitherto unknown but suspected realities of self— these all combine to create the rich perceptual fabric currently being activated within society. Mankind is being "turned on"—*made aware* of the existence of a reality it had never really expected to be real.

Mankind is learning of consciousness.

[1]*Babylon:* Biblical allegory term for the manufactured, imitation, seemingly naturally-existent physical reality in which all of mankind is unknowingly imprisoned.

216

# ESSAY 87

*Received August 26, 1984*

Perhaps the single most critical understanding yet to come involves the use of allegory within the scriptures—the Bible, the Book of Mormon, the Koran, etc. For it is with allegorical truths that the scriptures are written, and it is with literally interpreted fiction that they are understood, for not until the current time has there been released from the North Country any knowledge of the true content and meaning of the allegory of scriptures.

Allegory is, you see, a way of stating one thing in the guise of another; however, it is also a way therefore of hiding or concealing the true meaning within the enveloping literal or untrue interpretation or meaning it contains. The Bible and all scriptures of the North Country are almost entirely allegorical. Necessary because of the wide range of consciousness involved in mankind, allegory provides the possibility of literal lessons easily understood by a still-developing consciousness while simultaneously containing the allegorically derived truth for the benefit of the mature, advanced consciousness. Allegory is there-

217

THE SECOND BOOK OF THE LAMB

fore utilized extensively within scriptures, with virtually all meanings of allegorical truth concealed within literal elements or interpretations which may or may not be true in a factual sense. The lessons of scripture, you see, are the important message of the literal interpretations of scripture; factually true or not, the stories reveal powerful perceptive-awareness factors that mobilize and structure the developing perceptions of a growing, immature consciousness.

Beneath the largely fictional literal interpretations of scripture are the historical elements which confuse, confound, and solidify the apparent literal reality seemingly described. Combined in an artful way that produces allegory within the framework of detectable real historical events, the structure of scriptural allegory is advanced to the level whereby comprehension is achievable only by advanced or mature conscious beings. Graduates may then expect to determine the true meanings of scripture,[1] but the understanding will come slowly and arduously. Scripture describes, you see, a natural reality and order that is so far removed from your apparent reality and notions of scriptural content that the understandings must be given precept by precept—line by line. Only in that manner, and performed simultaneously with your transfiguration and unconfounding, will the true meaning of the scriptures and the wonders they contain be revealed to your inner understanding. But you *will* understand, and the understanding will be glorious.

*The Third Book of the Lamb* will evolve the understanding

---

[1]Compare Revelation 14:1-3 (reproduced in its entirety on p. 7): ". . . they sing a new song . . . . No one could learn that song except the hundred and forty-four thousand who had been redeemed from the earth."

of biblical lore; scriptures of all major lands will benefit from the wonders it reveals.

The past is behind, and a glorious future awaits the children of God.

# ESSAY 88

*Received September 17, 1984*

Needless to say, the state of readiness of planet earth approaches that of an army preparing for an objective to be taken, for it is in the extremely near future that the changes in society will occur as mankind learns and becomes fully aware of the reality in which it exists.

Mankind is, you see, about to embark on a journey unlike anything ever considered by the mind of man. Unfathomable reaches of awareness will open as mankind reaches for an attainable goal never before even imagined to exist. Almost too wonderful to hope for, the reality of man's future on earth is resplendent with the hope and joy of a species intimately involved with its Creator and with the knowledge of His love. Man will no longer wonder concerning the purpose of life, for he will *know,* and the knowledge will be glorious. Knowing, perceiving, *stretching* for one's own achievable godhood will become the star in each individual being's personal sky.

Dawn is breaking upon man, and with the dawn comes the light.

## ESSAY 89

*Received September 19, 1984*

Nonetheless, one can expect a monumental concussion upon the fabric of social interaction, with entire cultures revising their understood, perceived realities in the new light shed by my historic revelation of the true reality within which earth and mankind exist. Soon to be fully revealed and completely divulged to those of mankind, the natural reality exceeds all imagined or otherwise predicted characteristics of Heaven. All in the natural reality is love, creation, glory. God reigns supreme here, with love flowing through and from Him to all lesser organizations of consciousness in His cosmos. God *is* life, in the natural universe.

Placing oneself in the frame of reference or orientation of a muse, one can perhaps only just perceive the glorious future that awaits the new graduate of earth. Love, intellect, creation, glories in abundance—all await the newly matured child of God. His arms, and ours, are opened wide to receive you. He has waited since your very inception of consciousness, ages past, to welcome your completed, mature self to the natural realm He has prepared for all.

221

Those who have preceded you are eagerly awaiting your arrival and your bursting, unbounded joy at what you will soon perceive.

Welcome home, new graduate. Welcome to Heaven.

# AFTERWORD

All but the final two essays of this book were dictated by the Holy Ghost within a period of approximately seven weeks, with the entire work completed September 19, 1984, only eleven weeks after it began. For some reason known only in Heaven, however, he has intentionally restrained me—until now—from initiating the publication of both this book and *The First Book of the Lamb*, which was written before this work began.

In the intervening months he has continued the daily dictation. As briefly mentioned in the Preface, almost three thousand additional pages have been received thus far, each as increasingly informative and astounding as those you have just read. They further describe the nature of consciousness, the graduation and transfiguration process, scriptural allegory, and the source and cause of our physical reality. They describe the great signs and evidences that have been placed on earth, and tell of the major changes now being implemented in both man and society. They tell of a surrounding reality of beneficent beings with intellect beyond comprehension. They tell of what we are becoming and what we have always been.

The scriptural allegory information has now been completely received. It represents the single largest sign of the end of the age, for within it inherently lies not only the understanding of the signs, the covenants, and the prophecies, but the whole of scriptural antiquity. It reveals the underlying meanings of scripture while also illuminating the many codicils that have been incorporated by man. It provides the context needed by the scholar to rectify the many translation errors of ancient scripture. It reveals the unity of origin of all information intrusive to the physical system, for it underlies, as a common foundation, not only the Bible, the Book of Mormon, and the Koran, but modern spirit writings, the Dead Sea Scrolls, and the hidden, unsuspected message of a massive, ancient, sign of stone . . .

He will soon begin dictation of *The Third Book of the Lamb*, I am told. In addition, he has asked me to undertake the compilation of yet a fourth book that will describe the entirety of scriptural allegory in a single work. Then will follow additional steps of which I am yet unaware, as our future, the incredible purpose of our existence, and our very reality are spread before us like rare jewels on the sea of eternity.

Something very *wonderful* is happening!

Peter C. Stone
September 24, 1985

# INDEX

Abortion, 215-16
Abraham, 175
Allegory, biblical
  Abraham, Covenant with, 175
  ancient geographical locations and, 96
  Assyria, 166
  Babylon, 216$n$
  book on, 224
  Eden, garden of, 130
  Edom, 133, 165
  Flood, the, 114, 121-22
  further revelation of, 223-4
  generation, 103$n$
  "he who conquers," 180$n$
  Heaven, 22, 23$n$
  Hell, 163-64
  Medes, the, 159
  Moab, 165
  Noah, 114
  Noah's ark, 121
  North Country, 23$n$
  Satan, 162-64
  Sidon, 165

  structure of, 96-97, 217-18
  Tyre, 165
  See also individual allegorical terms.
Angel, fallen, 163
Animals, 204-5
Art, 104-8
Asexuality, 139
Assyria, 166

Babylon, 216$n$
Being, multidimensional, 81, 85-89, 92-95, 99-100, 193-94
Bible
  allegory of, 96-97, 217-19, 223-24
  origin of, 17
  purpose of, 35-36
  versions cited, 12
  See also Scriptures
Book of Mormon
  allegory of, 217-19, 224
  origin of, 17
  See also Scriptures

227

Books of the Lamb
  First, 12, 15-17, 181, 223
  publication of, 223-24
  Second, dictation of, 16-17,
    21, 34
  subsequent, 218-19, 224
Buddhism, 167
Bureaucracy, 165

Catholic Church, 166-67
Cause and effect, 132, 209
Christ, 15, 171-72, 181-83
Churches, seven. *See* Revelation
  to John
Churches, 90-91, 168, 197-99
  *See also* Religion
Communication
  brain functions for, 47
  as inner guidance, 180
  mass, 101-6
  mature, 169, 188
  prayer as, 200-201
  and separation of races, 114,
    116
  thought as, 32-33
  with graduates, 149, 152-3, 158
    with Holy Ghost, 15-17
Computers, 54
Confrontation, 189-91, 210-14
*Conquer*, 180n
Conscience, 40, 148
Consciousness
  advanced states of, 85-87,
    193-94
  of animals, 204-5
  asexuality of, 139
  characteristics of, 24, 37,
    99-100, 192-93
  entry and intermediate level,
    159-61, 166

  final integration of, 151-53,
    158
  images used in creation of,
    107-10
  integration into physical self,
    46, 110
  malcontent, 57-58
  in matter, 74
  origins of, 31, 204-5
  physical redistribution of,
    124, 129-31
  purpose of, 52, 192, 195
  sensory area of, 107
Cooker. *See* Stress crucible
Covenant with Abraham, 175
Creation, the, 143-44, 187-88
Creative force, primary
  control of, 84-85, 99
  images and, 109-10
  light and, 70
  love and, 25, 37, 185-86
  mass communication with,
    101-3, 105
  physical reality and, 123, 193
Cross, the, 90
Cycles of development, 97-98

Dead Sea Scrolls, 224
Death, physical, 94
Dictation, 16-17, 34
Dimensions
  as degrees of conscious
    freedom, 85, 88-89
  as higher planes of reality,
    141-44
  infinite, 85-88, 204
  physical perception of, 65-71,
    74, 142
  *See also* Being, multidimen-
    sional; Time; Relativity

Distance
  as intentional illusion, 81,
    88-89, 141-42
  interstellar, 69-72

Earth
  age of, 125-27, 130
  composition of, 70
  future of, 175-76, 178
  purpose of, 15, 22, 38, 145,
    177-78, 192
  revision of, 115-17, 120-24
Eden, garden of, 130
Edom, 90, 133, 165
Einstein, 77
Electrons, 65
Elohim, 188
Emotion, intrusive, 172, 188
Essays, sequence of, 125*n*
Evil
  knowledge of, 202
  purpose of, 162-64
Evolution, 112-15, 121-24
  *See also* Life forms

Fads, social, 103
Father, 182
*First Book of the Lamb, The*, 12,
  15-17, 181, 223
Firstborn, 180, 182
Flood, the
  ages prior to, 111-14, 125-27
  civilization prior to, 120
  consciousness redistribution,
    124, 129-31
  disease introduction, 131-33
  implementation of, 114-17,
    120-24
  natural laws and, 120-23
  stress policy following, 131-35

time alteration, 125-27
Force. *See* Creative force,
  primary
Fossils, 120

*Generation,* 103*n*
Generation(s)
  first, 116
  fourth, 103, 151, 172-75,
    177, 183-84
  future, 175-76
  third, 146, 168, 174, 183
  *See also* Graduates; Graduating
    class
Genetic processes, 110
God
  characteristics of, 52, 54, 144
  child of, 99, 149
  evolution of, 186-87
  force. *See* Creative force,
    primary
  higher authority, 52-53
  ignoring will of, 30-31, 57-58
  love of, 22, 40, 172, 177,
    185-86
  man's cultural awareness of, 39
  multidimensional perspective
    of, 85-87
  plan of, 22, 31, 171-78, 196
  realm of, 37
  Sons of. *See* Sons of God
  truth of, 119
  will of, 91, 161
Godhood
  achievable through growth,
    22, 31, 87, 185-86, 193-94
  perception of, 85-86
Government, 165
Graduates
  advanced capabilities of, 153

Graduates *(continued)*
  future of, 174-75, 177,
    221-22
  gathering of, 15, 150-51
  past, 116, 137-38, 146
  physical sensations of, 154-55
  unconfounding of, 146-55,
    157-58, 218
  understanding of, 27, 137,
    218
Graduating class, 97, 103, 146

"He who conquers," 180
Heaven, 22, 23$n$, 221-22
  *See also* Reality, natural
Hell, 163-64
"Hell on earth," 135
Holy Ghost, 15, 21, 173, 180, 183

Images
  artistic and musical, 105-8
  and creative processes, 84,
    107-10, 115, 123
  offspring, 110, 113
  physical reality and, 123
  stars as, 70, 156
Immortality
  of consciousness, 22, 24
  graduates and, 147
  mortality as illusion, 23
  as natural, 62-63
  *See also* Graduates,
    unconfounding of; Time,
    purpose of
Inner self, 101
Instinct, 102

Jesus, 168, 182
John the Baptist, 179, 182
Judaism, 167

Keys of the kingdom, 170
Knowing
  analogy, 55
  of graduates, 148, 153
  as mature mental process, 45,
    48, 94-95, 99-100
  as perception, 48, 59, 104
  physical senses and, 153$n$
  simulation of, 55
Koran
  allegory of, 217, 224
  origin of, 17
  *See also* Scriptures

Lamb, 15, 21, 171, 173, 180,
  182-83
Lamb, Books of the
  *See individual title*
Language, 114, 115
Life forms
  animal, 204-5
  criteria for, 111
  evolution of, 112-15,
    121-24
  lower, 102
  mammal, 116, 129
  micro-organic, 31, 131-32
  prehistoric, 111-12
  primate, 121, 124
Light
  nature of, 70
  speed of, 77
Love
  purpose of, 25
  force. *See* Creative force,
    primary
  graduates and, 154-55
  as growth-inducing tool, 128,
    130
  loss of, 139

in natural realm, 185-86,
        195-96
    teaching of, 129
Luther, Martin, 168

Malcontent, the, 57-58
Man
    continual improvement of,
        102-3
    control programs. *See*
        Programming
    future, 151, 159-61, 174-78,
        183-84, 202-3, 214, 220
    primal, 113-14
    races of, 114-15
    relationship to animals,
        204-5
    restructuring of, 115, 121-22,
        124
    life span of, 127
    physical design of, 46-47
    reproduction of, 110
    sexuality of, 139-40
Matter
    creation of, 109-10, 185,
        193
    as organization of creative
        force, 25, 75, 84
    revision of, 120-24
    *See also* Creation
Medes, 159-61
Medicine, 132-33, 166-67
Mental illness, 191
Metaphysics, 171
Moab, 90, 165
Moon, Reverend, 167
Mormonism, 167
Mortality, 23, 35
Motion pictures, 39, 216
Music, 104-8

Natural laws, 65, 67, 120
Nervous system, 112
Noah, 114
Noah's ark, 121
Non-information, 42-45, 117
North Country, 23$n$

Occult, 171

Pageant, 24
Perception
    development of, 42-51, 59-62,
        104-9, 189-91
    fundamental, 45
    invalid, 56
    nested levels of, 59-60
Planets, motion of the, 121
Politics, 171, 206-9
Prayer, 200-201
Prehistory, apparent, 120
Primates, 121, 124
Programming
    communicative, 46-47
    mass, 101-6, 159
    time, 65-69
Prophecy, 96-98

Race, 114, 115
Reality
    closed system of, 120-21, 132,
        142, 144, 209
    continual creation of, 144
    as corral, 51
    distance and, 81, 88-89, 92-93
    incremented, 76-81
    maintenance of, 185
    manufactured, 23-25
    natural, 83-86
    physical processes, 120-23
    source of, 223

231

Reality *(continued)*
  time and, 61-80, 125-27
  transcending physical, 146-47
  resolution of, 80
  *See also* Time; Creation
References cited, 12
Reincarnation
  as growth process, 29-31,
    145-46
  negative progress, 30-31, 58
  through species, 31, 204-5
Relativity, 69, 77-80
Religion(s)
  the clergy, 90-91, 197-99
  cult, 27
  eastern, 26, 29
  end of current, 179
  future, 171
  pageant and non-information
    in, 42-45
  purpose of, 26-28, 197-99
  as stress crucibles, 166-67
  western, 26
Reproduction, 110, 139-40
Revelation to John, the
  as allegory, 96
  meaning of, 179-80
  stars, fall of the, 172
  thousand years, the, 98
  white stone, 149
Rock music, 103

Sacraments, 91
Salvation, 90
Satan, 162-64
Science, 132, 143-44, 165, 171
Scriptures
  allegory of, 96, 217-19,
    223-24
  and intermediate truth, 35-36

pageants of, 41-44
purpose of, 35-36
source of, 17, 21, 34, 169
transcending guidance of,
  36
translation errors of, 224
*Second Book of the Lamb, The,*
  dictation of, 16-17, 21, 34
  publication of, 223
Sequence of essays, 125n
Sexes, 139-40
Sidon, 165
Signs and evidences, 223
Sin, 202
Social evolution, 135, 159-61,
  206-9
Social fads, 103
Sons of God
  creation of, 111, 187
  role of, 34, 169-70, 175, 180,
    183, 187-88
Soul. *See* Consciousness
Space, 81, 88, 93, 141-42
Space travel, 72
Species. *See* Life forms;
  Reincarnation
Spirit writings, 224
Stars
  as images, 70, 156, 172
  fall of the, 172
  motion of the, 121
Stress
  confrontation, 189-91, 210-14
  consciousness development
    using, 113-17, 128-38,
    165-66
  illness and disease, 131-33
  major lifetime episodes of,
    137
Stress crucible, 134

*Third Book of the Lamb, The,*
218-19, 224
Thought processes
as communication, 32-33
mature, 95
*See also* Knowing
Time
alteration of, 121, 125-27
composite of advanced
dimensions, 88
as function of current
perceptive ability, 77
as function of growth
processes, 64
as intentional illusion, 69-74,
142
Paradox, the, 73
past, 73
perception of, 64-66
purpose of, 61-63, 125-26
quantitative, 77
relativity and, 78-80
subsequent realities, 67-68,
76, 126

Transfiguration. *See* Graduate,
unconfounding of
Truth
and frames of reference, 97,
118-19, 181
intermediate, 27-28, 35, 157
Tyre, 165

UFO's, 216
Universe
closed, 141
design of, 142
interstellar distances of, 70
parallel, 82
scientific understanding of,
144, 156

Violence, 213

War, 210-13
White stone, 149
Will, free, 207